The Story of THE BLUE NILE

ALAN MOOREHEAD

The Story of THE BLUE NILE

An abridgment by Lucy Moorehead
of THE BLUE NILE

HARPER & ROW, PUBLISHERS
NEW YORK

THE STORY OF THE BLUE NILE

 For information address Harper & Row, Publishers, Incorporated, 49 East 33rd Street, New York 16, N. Y.

Library of Congress Catalog Card Number: 66–15679

Contents

ILLUSTRATIONS

ILLUSTRATIONS

The endpapers, taken from a sketch by Denon, depict the Battle of the Pyramids. Reproduced by kind permission of Hamish Hamilton, Ltd., London.

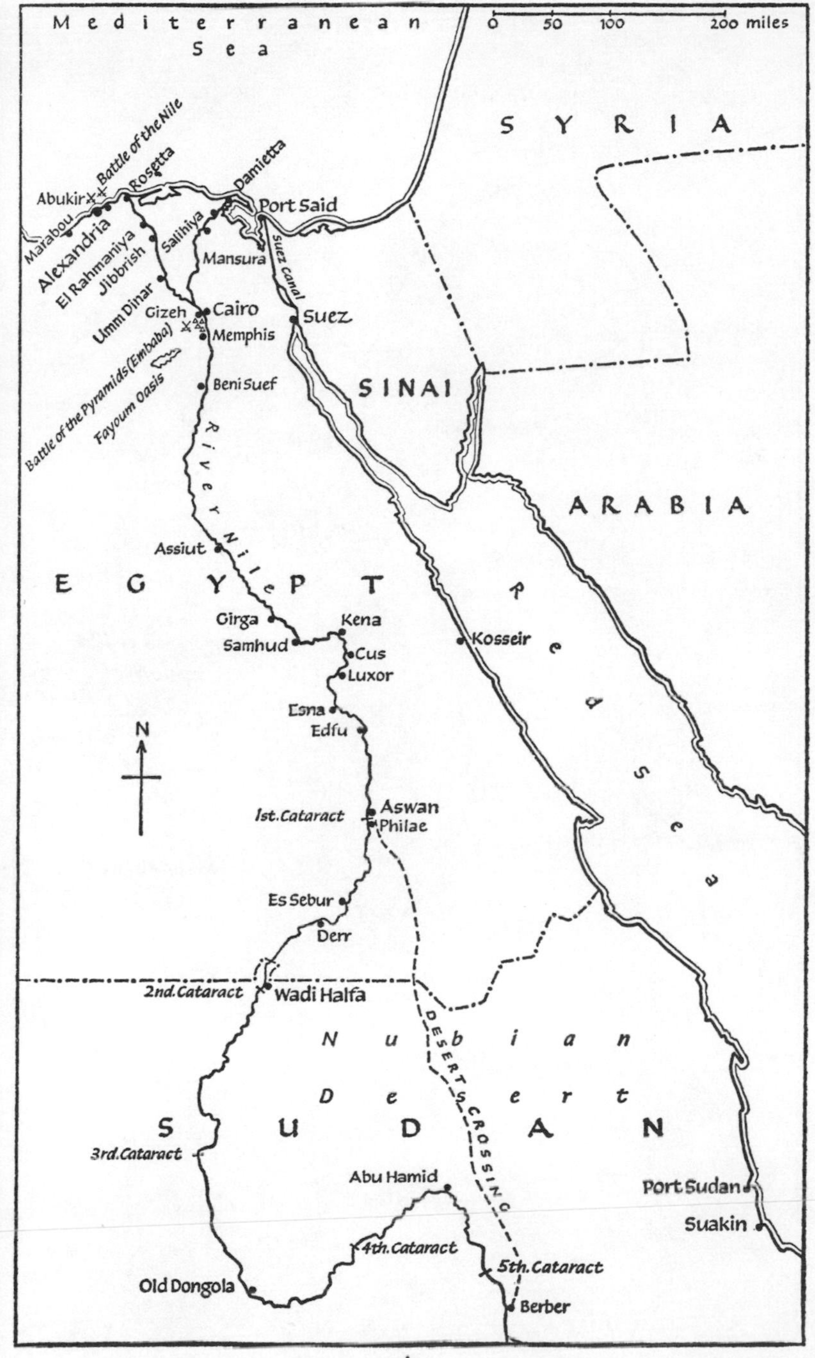
Mediterranean Sea
0 50 100 200 miles
SYRIA
Battle of the Nile
Rosetta
Damietta
Abukir
Port Said
Marabou
Alexandria
El Rahmaniya
Jibbrish
Salihiya
Mansura
Suez Canal
Umm Dinar
Gizeh
Cairo
Suez
Memphis
Battle of the Pyramids (Embaba)
Fayoum Oasis
Beni Suef
SINAI
River Nile
ARABIA
Assiut
EGYPT
Red Sea
Girga
Kena
Samhud
Cus
Kosseir
Luxor
Esna
Edfu
N
1st. Cataract
Aswan
Philae
Es Sebur
Derr
2nd. Cataract
Wadi Halfa
Nubian Desert
DESERT CROSSING
SUDAN
3rd. Cataract
Abu Hamid
Port Sudan
Suakin
4th. Cataract
5th. Cataract
Old Dongola
Berber

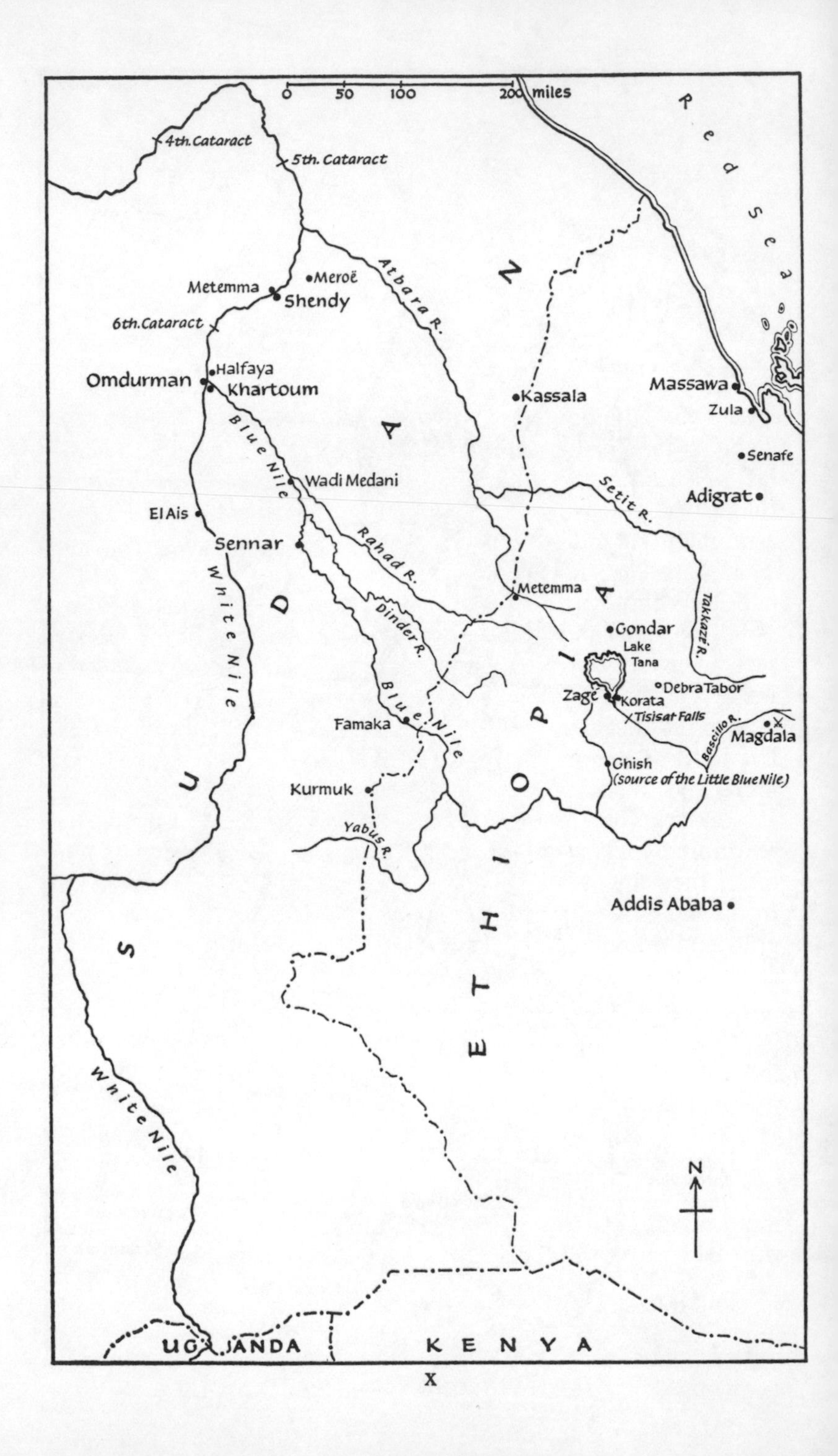
0
50
100
200 miles
Red Sea
4th. Cataract
5th. Cataract
6th. Cataract
Meroë
Metemma
Shendy
Halfaya
Omdurman
Khartoum
Atbara R.
Kassala
Massawa
Zula
Senafe
Adigrat
Setit R.
Blue Nile
Wadi Medani
El Ais
Sennar
Rahad R.
White Nile
Dinder R.
Metemma
Gondar
Lake Tana
Takkazé R.
Zage
Korata
Debra Tabor
Tisisat Falls
Bascillo R.
Magdala
Famaka
Blue Nile
Ghish
(source of the Little Blue Nile)
Kurmuk
Yabus R.
Addis Ababa
SUDAN
ETHIOPIA
White Nile
N
UGANDA
KENYA

CHAPTER ONE

THE TWO NILES

THE Blue Nile pours very quietly and uneventfully out of Lake Tana in the northern highlands of Ethiopia. There is no waterfall or cataract, no definite current, nothing in fact to indicate that a part at least of this gently moving flow is embarked upon a momentous journey to the Mediterranean, 2,750 miles away. There are no villages here, and except for a few fishermen paddling about on their papyrus rafts like water-boatmen in a pond, no sign of civilization at all. The silence is absolute. One sees a few spry grey monkeys on the rocks, and the black and white kingfisher, fluttering ten feet above the water before he makes his dead-straight drop upon a fish. Pythons are said to live in these regions, and they grow to a length of twenty feet or more and are adorned in patterns of black and many colors. If you are very lucky you might catch sight of one of them swimming to new hunting grounds along the shore, but more often they are to be found in the low branches of trees, and from that safe hiding place among the leaves they lash out to grab and demolish a monkey or a small unsuspecting antelope coming down to the river to drink.

We are here 6,000 feet above the level of the sea, and the equatorial sunshine is immensely hot and bright. A few miles downstream from the lake the water begins to boil turbulently over rocks and shallows which are impossible to navigate with any safety; and so the traveler must take to mules and follow the river as close to its banks as the thick scrub will allow him.

The landscape is delightful, a combination of tropical and mountainous Africa: acacia trees and the lotus, the banyan and the alien eucalyptus, palms and delicate water-ferns. We are as yet a little too far upstream for the crocodile, but there is an exuberance of birds: the fish eagle calling from the treetop in the morning, white storks with a delicate fringe of black on the wings, starlings that look like anything but starlings since their feathers gleam with an iridescent blue, the black ibis with its scimitar beak, pelicans, darters, hoopoes, rollers and kites; and the giant hornbill which is the size of a young ostrich and rather more ungainly until it lumbers into the air, and then reveals the great sweep of its wings, each tipped with white.

The eastern bank is a succession of rough hills, but on the west black cotton-soil plains spread away to distant mountains which are very strange: their tops are the granite cores of extinct volcanoes and they sprout like vast grey cactuses in the sky.

After about twenty miles of this one is aware of some sort of commotion ahead. The murmur of the water grows into a roar, and a low wet cloud hangs over the valley. This is the great object of this stage of your journey, the Tisisat Falls, and it is an extraordinary thing that they should be so little known, for they are, by some way, the grandest spectacle that either the Blue or the White Nile has to offer; in all Africa they are only to be compared with the Victoria Falls on the Zambezi. As with the Victoria Falls, there is the same calm approach past small wooded islands and smooth rocks, and then abruptly the stream vanishes in a tremendous white downpour that thunders as it falls. Looking down from the top one sees far below a narrow gorge filled with racing water, and it twists and turns until it is finally lost to sight in the surrounding cliffs. The spray flung up from this gorge creates a perpetual soft rain which is blown upon the hillside opposite, and here a forest of wet green reeds keeps waving from side to side like seaweed at the bottom of the sea. To stand there just for five minutes means that you will be wet to the skin. For the newcomer it is an alarming sort of place, and he will see with surprise flocks of little black birds with pointed pinkish wings flying directly into the spray and landing on the slippery rocks at the very lip where the water makes its frightful downward plunge. Unconcerned they fly off again through a rainbow which is nearly circular and which hangs in the spray like a whirling firework.

The Tisisat Falls are the end of all peace on the Blue Nile. The river now begins to make its great gash through the Ethiopian plateau. For nearly four hundred miles it continues in an immense curve, at first in a southerly direction, then west, then north, until it pours itself out of the mountains into the hot plains of the south Sudan. The further it goes the deeper it cuts; by the time it reaches central Ethiopia the gorge is a mile deep and at places fifteen miles wide, yet still, even at the height of the dry season, it tears and boils along too fast for any boat to live upon the surface. No one has ever made the boat journey down the Blue Nile from Lake Tana to the Sudan, no one as yet has managed to walk or take a mule along the full length of its precipitous banks.

The Blue Nile joins the White Nile at Khartoum. The White Nile is a much longer river than the Blue. Already at Khartoum it has come two thousand miles from its source in Lake Victoria in Central Africa, and except for its passage through the great swamp of the Sudd in the south Sudan its banks are inhabited nearly all the way. However, the real strength of the two rivers that now unite and lose their separate identity at Khartoum lies in the Blue Nile. It provides six-sevenths of the total volume of water in the combined stream, and for six months of the year it rushes down from the Ethiopian mountains with the effect of a tidal wave. By June the force of this flood is so great that the White Nile is dammed back upon itself at Khartoum; it pauses, as it were, and stands back while the younger, livelier river pushes past carrying hundreds of thousands of tons of discoloring grit and soil to Egypt. At last in January the tremendous rush subsides, and the White Nile begins to assert itself again. Then at Khartoum you can see the two rivers flowing on quietly side by side, and for a few miles there is a distinct dividing line between them on the surface of the water: the White Nile not precisely white but more nearly muddy grey, the Blue seldom absolutely blue except for certain moments at dawn and in the evening, but more of a brownish-green.

The river still has another 1,750 miles to go before it reaches the Mediterranean, and it will receive only one more tributary, the Atbara—another gift of the Lake Tana highlands—before it plunges into regions where there is no rain at all, nothing but this warm, brown, softly moving flow of water to relieve the endless sameness of the desert.

Finally the Nile begins to drop its Ethiopian mud at Cairo, a hundred miles from the sea. Confused by flatness and its own tame pace, it spreads out through many different canals and waterways into the green fan of the delta. Little by little with its falling silt it has pushed the land out into the Mediterranean and lost itself in swamps and lakes. Of the seven mouths the ancients knew only two remain, one at Rosetta and the other at Damietta, but still at the height of its flood the river stains the sea for many miles out, and in a storm coming from the north russet waves are driven back on to the Egyptian shore.

This, then, is the end of the river, the end of a continuous chain of re-creation by which the Blue Nile brings life down from the mountains to the desert and the delta. Without it the people of Egypt and of a great part of the Sudan could not exist for a single day. Even a 'low Nile'—an annual flood that has been less than average—is a disaster. This has always been so and is likely to continue forever. It seems astonishing, therefore, that so little was known about the river to the outside world in comparatively recent times. As late as 1770 the White Nile was an utter mystery, and it was not even generally accepted that the river had not one source but two. Most of the great temples on the lower Nile were buried in sand, and in the ramshackle mud-hut villages that perched on the river bank life went by in a torpor of ignorance and monotony. For well over a thousand years the great civilization of ancient Egypt had been forgotten and its writings were a closed book; nor did there appear to be any bright prospects for the future.

Clearly this detachment and stagnation could not last. It could only be a short time before the aggressive curiosity of Europe was drawn irresistibly towards Africa; before Egypt, the Sudan and Ethiopia were each in turn invaded by foreign armies, and the river and its tremendous past were reopened to the outside world. In 1774 news arrived from the most unexpected and least accessible quarter of all—from the heart of Ethiopia itself. James Bruce declared that he had been to the very source of the Blue Nile and had traced its course from Lake Tana to the sea. It was a kind of reconnaissance for the great upheaval that lay ahead.

CHAPTER TWO

JAMES BRUCE AT THE SOURCE

EVEN by the standards of his time and his class Bruce was a formidable man. He was six foot four in height and strong in proportion, and he had dark red hair and a very loud voice. He had a reputation as a horseman and a marksman, and wherever he went he seems to have dispensed an air of confident superiority. He felt superior. Even Arabic and the Ethiopian dialects did not defeat his natural fluency in languages, he was an enthusiastic amateur of such subjects as astronomy, he was socially at ease and he was rich. If he was quick to take offense (he describes himself as of "a sanguine, passionate disposition, very sensible of injuries"), and was often childishly vain and boastful, he was also a man of imagination, and there is no doubt whatever that he was very brave and very determined.

He was born on the family estates of Kinnaird in Scotland in 1730, and within three years his mother had died. His father soon married again and had three daughters and six sons by his second wife. Thus from the first Bruce remained a little apart from the rest of the family as the eldest son by another wife, and the heir to property and privileges which dated back, it was claimed, to the ancient kings of Scotland. He was a delicate child who soon outgrew his own strength, yet at the age of six he was sent to be educated by tutors in London, a week's journey away by coach to the south. At the age of twelve he was put into Harrow school, where they thought very well of him as a scholar. Education 200 years ago was pushed ahead much more rapidly and thoroughly than it is today, and at sixteen Bruce was sent back to Scotland to continue his studies at Edinburgh University.

By the time he was twenty-four he had studied Arabic manuscripts in Spain, he had sailed down the Rhine, he had fought a duel in Brussels, he had made drawings of ruins in Italy, and eventually George III's ministers found him a job as British consul among the Barbary pirates in Algiers. It was not an easy post. Ali Pasha, the Bey of Algiers, was a cruel old man who thought nothing of throwing foreign consuls into jail and of enslaving the crews of visiting ships. Bruce presumably knew what he was in for but already he had vague plans for getting to the source of the Nile—that mystery which for 2,000 years had been, he declared, "a defiance of all travelers, and an opprobrium to geography"—and Algiers was a step along the way. In June 1762, aged thirty-two, he arrived at Algiers equipped with two camera obscuras for drawing ruins and a quantity of astronomical instruments to chart his journeys in Africa. He found things much worse than he could have anticipated: the Bey was furious at the seizure of one of his ships by the British and the French and was out for blood. Within the first few months of his consulship Bruce saw the French consul taken away in chains, Forbes, his own assistant, was threatened with "a thousand bastinadoes" and fled into hiding, and Bruce himself scarcely dared to go out. When he did have an audience with the Bey one of the court officials was strangled in his presence. Bruce stuck it for two years before the British Government gave him permission to leave his post and continue with his journey to the east.

The year 1768, when he was thirty-eight, finds him in Cairo accompanied by a young Italian secretary named Luigi Balugani, and dressed as a dervish. And now at last he has his great design in view: he will travel up the Nile into the unknown fastnesses of Ethiopia.

There are a number of unusual aspects about the tremendous journey upon which Bruce now embarked. Like Marco Polo he tells an intensely personal story, and the people he writes about so confidently and familiarly were then as strange to Europe and the civilized world as the denizens of outer space are to us today. On his return, says his biographer, Francis Head, he told the public "of people who wore rings in their lips instead of their ears—who anointed themselves not with bear's grease or pomatum, but with the blood of cows—who, instead of playing tunes upon them, wore the entrails of animals as ornaments—and who, instead of eating hot putrid meat, licked their lips over bleeding living flesh. He told of men who hunted each other and he described crowds of human beings and huge animals retreating in terror before an army of little flies! In short, he told them the truth, the whole truth, and nothing but the truth; but . . . the facts he related were too strong."

There was yet another impediment to the success of Bruce's journey. He was absolutely fixed in the mistaken idea that the Blue Nile was the main stream and that the White Nile was a tributary. However, this scarcely mattered; every journey in Africa at this time added something to human knowledge, and the Blue Nile was every bit as important as the White.

In November 1769 he turned towards the interior. Up to this point he had covered ground which was dangerous but fairly well explored. Now he faced the unknown.

There were about twenty men in the little party. Six asses had also been bought in Massawa, but Bruce himself walked. In three weeks he had crossed the coastal plain and had struggled up the mountain paths to Adowa, which was then a place of some 300 houses and one of the principal strongholds of the country. Here Bruce had a warning of what lay before him: several hundred miserable wretches were imprisoned in cages awaiting the day when their families could raise enough money to buy their release.

In mid-February 1770, ninety-five days out of Massawa, the party reached Gondar, and Bruce settled into a house in the Muslim quarter. Addis Ababa at this time had not yet been built, and Gondar was the principal city of the country. It was a settlement of some 10,000 families who lived in clay huts with conical roofs, but the King's palace was a large square building flanked by towers and a surrounding wall. It had a view down to Lake Tana, and its principal reception hall was 120 feet long. For most of the year, however, the court lived in tents and followed the army on its endless meanderings across the Ethiopian plateau.

The young King, Tecla Haimanout, and his vizier Ras Michael, who really ruled the country, were away on one of their punitive raids when Bruce arrived, and so he paid court to the Iteghe, the queen mother. She seems to have been an intelligent woman. "See! See!" she exclaimed one day to Bruce when he confided to her the object of his journey, "how every day our life furnishes us with proofs of the perverseness and contradiction of human nature: you are come from Jerusalem, through vile Turkish governments, and hot, unwholesome climates, to see a river and a bog, no part of which can you carry away were it ever so valuable, and of which you have in your own country a thousand larger, better and cleaner... While I, on the other hand, the mother of kings, who have sat upon the throne of this country more than thirty years, have for my only wish, night and day, that after giving up everything in the world, I could be conveyed to the church of the Holy Sepulchre in Jerusalem, and beg alms for my subsistence all my life after, if I could only be buried at last in the street within sight of the gate of that temple where our blessed Savior once lay."

Her daughter, Ozoro Esther, who was married to Ras Michael, also attracted Bruce's sympathy, for she was a beautiful girl and she was driven half-mad by the violence around her. Hardly so much could be said for Tecla Haimanout and Ras Michael; when Bruce first met them they were busy putting out the eyes of a dozen captives. Of the King's appearance Bruce tells us very little, but Ras Michael emerges as a fairly well-defined figure, a terrible, white-haired old tyrant in his seventies, who adopted the airs and manners of a medieval baron. He rode into Gondar wearing a cloak of black velvet with a silver fringe, a page marching at his right stirrup carrying a silver wand. Behind him came the army, each soldier who had killed a man bearing on his lance a shred of scarlet cloth.

Bruce was received in audience a day or two later, and he found Michael sitting on a sofa, surrounded by his followers, his hair hanging in short curls, a gaunt, authoritative figure, about six foot in height, with very intelligent eyes. Bruce made the customary obeisance by kissing the ground at his feet and was well received. After warning him of the dangers of moving about the country alone, Michael gave him the command of a troop of the King's horse.

It is wonderful that Bruce should have survived and have even been honored among these violent men whose first instinct was to kill a stranger and then rob him of his goods. He had a certain value as an oddity, of course, and he carried with him a formidable portfolio of letters from the Sultans in Constantinople, Cairo and Mecca, but they hardly counted for much in this barbaric Christian world. He tells us that the Ethiopian warriors were greatly impressed by the power of his modern rifle, especially when he galloped about on a black charger potting at the mountain kites. His skill as a doctor also made him very welcome, since plagues like smallpox were common, and it was useful that he had learned to speak both Geez and Arabic. But in the end probably it was his commanding presence and his air of assurance that really saved his life. Explorers in Africa tend to fall into two groups: those who absorbed the protective local coloring of the country and who went about in disguise pretending to be merchants, couriers or even pilgrims on their way to Mecca; and the practical men who boldly announced their identity and who disarmed opposition by marching ahead to their objectives with a show of perfect confidence. Bruce was no fool in the arts of persuasion, and he tells us that in Ethiopia he got himself up in chain mail, cloaks and bright cummerbunds stuck with pistols like any other chieftain, but he tends on the whole to belong to the practical group. He also possessed a good eighteenth-century knowledge of court intrigue and the soft word that induces patronage. "Man is the same creature everywhere although different in color," he wrote. "The court in London and that in Abyssinia[1] are in their principles the same."

[1] Although Ethiopia is more correct, the term Abyssinia was in general use at this time.

And so, when he had cleared the queen mother's palace of smallpox and had flirted with Ozoro Esther and had flattered Ras Michael, they were ready enough to take him off on the next expedition at the south of Lake Tana, where a rebel chief named Fasil was raising an army against the throne.

This was precisely the direction in which Bruce wanted to go, and it was a great disappointment to him that Fasil should have surrendered before he could get to the Little Abbai, which he believed to be the true source of the Nile. He did, however, reach the river close to its outflow from Lake Tana, and here he turned southeast to the Tisisat Falls. "The cataract itself," he says, "was the most magnificent sight that I ever beheld. The height has been rather exaggerated. The missionaries say the fall is about sixteen ells, or fifty feet. The measuring is indeed very difficult; but by the position of long sticks, and poles of different lengths, at different heights of the rock, from the water's edge, I may venture to say, that it is nearer forty feet than any other measure. The river had been considerably increased by rains, and fell in one sheet of water, without any interval, above half an English mile in breadth, with a force and noise that was truly terrible, and which stunned, and made me, for a time, perfectly dizzy. It was a magnificent sight that ages, added to the greatest length of human life, would not efface or eradicate from my memory; it struck me with a kind of stupor, and a total oblivion of where I was, and of every other sublunary concern. It was one of the most magnificent, stupendous sights in the creation."

The passage is revealing; in fact, it provides a valuable key, not only to Bruce's nature but also to the account of his journey which he was eventually to publish in England. There is first of all his inaccuracy, and it is very puzzling. One cannot altogether blame him for exalting the scene before him—after all, most of the explorers were guilty of exaggeration, and the Tisisat Falls are indeed very fine. But such phrases as "one of the most magnificent, stupendous sights in the creation" are perhaps a little too much; they smack of the storyteller and the supernatural. Then when he gets down to facts he makes the Falls much wider than they really are, but less than a third of their true height; the actual drop is not forty feet but a hundred and fifty.

Bruce returned with the army to the intrigues at Gondar and the mutilation and massacre of the prisoners there. For a while he was ill with fever (no doubt malaria), and it was not until October 1770 that he was able to set out again. This time he traveled with his own small party. For the moment the country was at peace, and Bruce had so far got himself into the good graces of the King and Ras Michael that he had been nominated governor of Ghish, the territory around the source of the Little Abbai. Bruce had neither the means nor the intention of residing there, but it provided a sort of passport for his journey, and it enabled him to impress the local chieftains he met along the way. He passed around the west side of Lake Tana and then moved up the valley of the Little Abbai towards Ghish Mountain, which is about seventy miles south of the lake. The final march was made on November 4, 1770, through charming country filled with flowering shrubs and tropical birds and with a view of vast mountains in the distance. Late in the afternoon, when they had climbed to 9,500 feet, they came on a rustic church, and the guide, pointing beyond it, indicated a little swamp with a hillock rising from the center; that, he declared, was the source of the Nile.

"Throwing my shoes off," Bruce says, "I ran down the hill, towards the little island of green sods, which was about two hundred yards distant; the whole side of the hill was thick overgrown with flowers, the large bulbous roots of which appearing over the surface of the ground, and their skins coming off on treading upon them, occasioned me two very severe falls before I reached the brink of the marsh; I after this came to the island of green turf, which was in the form of an altar . . . and I stood in rapture. . . ."

There was no actual flow to be seen—the water merely appeared to seep through the swamp from several different springs to a point on its downward side where it combined into a tiny brook—but there was clear, cold water in the well and to Bruce at that moment it was sacred.

"It is easier to guess than to describe the situation of my mind at the moment," he says, "standing in that spot which had baffled the genius, industry and inquiry of both ancients and moderns, for the course of near three thousand years.... Though a mere private Briton, I triumphed here in my own mind, over kings and their armies."

But then, almost at once, he tells us, a reaction set in. For well over a year through tremendous hardships and dangers he had struggled to reach this goal, and now suddenly, having won the battle, having achieved what had so often seemed impossible, the impetus and the inspiration of his journey were gone; now he faced the long way home. "I found," he says, "a despondency gaining ground fast upon me, and blasting the crown of laurels I had woven for myself."

Determined to be merry, Bruce picked up a half coconut shell he used as a drinking cup. Filling it from the spring he drank a toast to "His Majesty King George III and a long line of princes."

It was a strange scene, full of delusions. If Bruce was looking for the source of the Nile he was on the wrong river. The true source was in Lake Victoria, a thousand miles away. He was even on the wrong part of the wrong river.

There was an even more serious delusion than this: Bruce was utterly mistaken in thinking that he was the first European to reach this spot. Pedro Paez, a Portuguese priest, had been here in 1618, and his account of his experiences is very clear and very similar to Bruce's.

It is useless for Bruce to claim as he did that all Paez's distances and place-names are wrong, and that Paez's whole account is based upon hearsay. There can be no doubt whatever that Paez had been here 150 years earlier, and Bruce's attack was both spiteful and ungenerous. This was a pity, because Bruce was to make a tremendous contribution to the knowledge of the Nile and of northeast Africa, he was a genuine pioneer, and he had no need to filch others' spoils or discredit their reputation. He in his turn was soon to know the full bitterness of such unfairness when it was directed upon himself.

The whole argument, of course, is very trivial—who really cared about this discovery of a remote spring in Ethiopia?—and yet it was true that from Cyrus to Julius Caesar the kings of the ancient world had occupied themselves with this matter in vain; and it is also true that the history of the river is compounded not out of calm deductions and wise decisions but out of just such petty disputes and jealousies as this. It is a story that unfolds through rivalry, pride, greed and finally bloodshed. "Peace," Richard Burton says somewhere, quoting an old proverb, "is the dream of the wise, war is the history of man."

CHAPTER THREE

DISBELIEF AT HOME

AFTER spending four days at Ghish to complete his observations Bruce returned to Gondar, to find that during his absence the whole country had abandoned itself to civil war. There was no possibility of his returning home while the hostilities were going on, and so he threw himself into the fray with the others and helped his friends where he could. It was a valuable period: as month after month went by he was able to observe the Ethiopians more closely than any contemporary European had ever done. He went to great pains over the study of their history, and his list of the kings of Ethiopia is one of the few authentic documents on the subject that we have. He made collections of original manuscripts and of plants and minerals, he kept daily meteorological recordings ("Smart showers in the evening and night; inches .342," runs a typical entry: it was always raining), and his general notes are full of interest. He relates that the fish in the Lake Tana waters were caught by being drugged and that in the Lake itself there were forty-five inhabited islands—"If you believe the Abyssinians, who, in everything are very great liars . . . dissimulation in all ranks of these people is as natural as breathing." Bruce himself thought there were eleven islands. He says that the lake was too cold for crocodiles, but that he observed many "river-horses" in addition to deer, buffaloes, boars and hyenas so ferocious that they would drag a donkey down in the night and even attack a man.

At last in December 1771, over two years since his first arrival in the country, Bruce got permission to go. He chose the long inland route that led down from the mountains to

Metemma and the deserts of the Sudan and thence along the valley of the Nile to Cairo.

He left in surprisingly good order with three Greeks and a gang of porters, well mounted on horses and baggage animals, and he carried with him in addition to his quadrant and his collections a gold chain given him by the court, and a quantity of cloth and other goods with which to buy off the predatory local chieftains along the way. He was now forty-one, and a diet of raw meat and honey had not impaired his strength in the least. On the way down to Metemma he delayed for a while to go off elephant hunting, but the hot malarial foothills and the empty desert were very nearly his undoing: he came down with fever for two months and some of his followers died of thirst. With the end of the wet season the tsetse fly, which was fatal to domestic animals, was driving everything before it, and Bruce's small party was a very easy prey for the warlike sheikhs along the route; more than once he was very nearly murdered. Eventually, at the end of April 1772, four months after leaving Gondar, the little band crossed the Dinder and Rahad rivers and struggled into Sennar.

It was the worst time of the year in Sennar, and Bruce's description of it is depressing: "No horse, mule, ass, or any beast of burden, will breed, or even live at Sennar, or many miles around it. Poultry does not live there. Neither dog nor cat, sheep nor bullock, can be preserved a season there . . . Two greyhounds which I brought from Atbara, and the mules which I had brought from Abyssinia, lived only a few weeks after I arrived."

Bruce hated Sennar and fled from it as soon as he could get away, but before that happened, in September 1772, he was mulcted of nearly all the goods he had brought with him from Ethiopia. Even his gold chain was taken away from him, and but six links of it remained to him to pay his way down two thousand miles of the river to Cairo. Within a week or two he arrived on camels at the junction of the two Niles at Halfaya, "a large, handsome and pleasant town, although built with clay." It stood further back from the river than the present city of Khartoum, and he noted that the inhabitants ate cats, crocodiles and river-horses. Of the White Nile, however, he says barely a word. One can almost see him turning his head away from it; how unbearable after so many years of danger and hardship to admit the thought that his own stream, the Blue Nile in Ethiopia, could have a rival. He allows that the White Nile is larger than the Blue, but he refuses to call it the Nile at all—he refers to it by its native name, the Abiad. One sympathizes.

He was now growing very tired, and to add to his discomfort he contracted the nilotic disease of guinea worm, which is a parasite that eats into the flesh. However, on October 4 he reached Shendy and now at last he was in touch with the outside world. From this point caravans set out fairly regularly for Cairo. The village at this time had been reduced to a bare twenty-five houses but the market was flourishing—goods were much cheaper and better than they were at Sennar—and Bruce was aware that he had reached a very ancient settlement on the Nile. For the first time since he had been in Axum in Ethiopia three years before, he came upon the relics of ruined temples. Outside Shendy "heaps of broken pedestals and pieces of obelisks" covered with hieroglyphics were strewn in the desert. His route did not take him past the pyramids that lay nearby but he noted in his journal: "It is impossible to avoid risking a guess that this is the ancient city of Meroë," and his guess was perfectly right.

Curiously he does not mention Shendy castle but during his two weeks' stay he paid court to the Sittina, the queen of the province who lived about half a mile outside the town.

She sat behind a screen when she first received Bruce but he induced her to emerge on his second visit and he beheld a tall beautiful woman of forty with very red lips and the finest teeth and eyes he had ever seen. She was dressed in a purple stole with a magnificent gold crown on her head and her plaited hair fell below her waist; and to Bruce she seemed a living reincarnation of the legendary Queen Candace who had ruled Meroë and all the Nile north to Egypt in the times of the Pharaohs. He kissed her hand and the Queen, starting back, exclaimed that such a thing had never happened to her before. All through this month—October 1772—a strange light glowed in the sky. "The planet Venus," Bruce says, "appeared shining with undiminished light all day, in defiance of the brightest sun"—a statement that seems hardly credible although indeed Venus did, that year, approach very close to the earth.[1]

At the end of October he moved on again. He crossed the Atbara, the Nile's last tributary, which he found at this season to be a quarter of a mile wide and very deep, and at Berber he paused to rest and buy more camels before setting out on the fearsome caravan route that ran directly across the desert to Aswan. This was a journey of some 400 miles, but it was infinitely shorter than the alternative route that followed the river on its great loop around to the west.

There was a final visit to the river bank—"I bathed myself with infinite pleasure for a long half hour in the Nile; and thus took leave of my old acquaintance, very doubtful if we should ever meet again"—and on November 11, 1772, Bruce and eight men "committed themselves to the desert." It was said by later travelers that Bruce greatly exaggerated the horrors of this crossing, especially in his account of the "simoon," the blasting wind that gathers up the sand in columns like waterspouts in the sky. "Silence," he says, "and a desperate kind of indifference about life were the immediate effect upon us." Yet it is only fair to remember that he had only recently come from the mountains, and that quite possibly he may have struck a particularly severe heat wave. One of his men went mad and was abandoned. His camels died, and the quadrant, along with the rest of his baggage, had to be left behind. He himself went lame with blistered feet, and in addition they were constantly fighting off marauding Arabs around the water wells. At last on November 28, like sailors who know from the appearance of floating driftwood that land is near, they saw river-birds in the sky, and the following morning they dragged themselves into Aswan. The crossing had taken eighteen days.

Bruce was now virtually back in civilization, since from here on the Mameluke government of Egypt was in control, and he

[1] Captain Cook had been sent to Tahiti in the Pacific to observe it.

still carried his pass from the Bey in Cairo. The governor of Aswan was helpful. Bruce recovered his abandoned baggage from the desert, and on December 11 he set sail down the river to Cairo. A month later, dressed like a beggar, feeling ill, and exhausted and suffering great pain from his feet, he arrived in Cairo. Here he recuperated for two months, and by the time he sailed for Europe in March 1773, only the guinea worm was troubling him; on being drawn out of his knee it had broken off and had retreated into his leg again. He landed in Marseilles after a three weeks' voyage.

In the spring of 1774 he crossed from Paris to London. At first things went well. The learned societies and the salons of fashionable London were very ready to hear what Bruce had to say. It was soon apparent, however, that they were listening, not with respect, but with amusement; the sort of amusement one reserves for marvelous storytellers. What on earth was all this about cutting steaks from cows? And how droll the good man was about his barbarous emperors and sheikhs, his girl-brides, his black slaves and his river-horses.

There can hardly have been a time when London could produce so many wits to deal with this sort of thing. Peter Pindar, the fashionable satirist of the day, was soon to compose a couplet:

Nor have I been where men (what loss alas!)
Kill half a cow and turn the rest to grass.

It was all too good to be true.

There is even a slight note of derision from the writer Fanny Burney, who also met Bruce about this time. She wrote: "Mr. Bruce's grand air, gigantic height, and forbidding brow awed everybody. He is the tallest man you ever saw without paying."

Bruce was affronted and disgusted. "As soon as Bruce found," his biographer says, "that in England public opinion was against him, in sullen indignation, he determined to retire into his own country . . . his spirit too proud to accept a smile as an atonement for a barbarous prejudice and an unjustifiable insult."

Edinburgh received him better, and so did Bruce's own

estates at Kinnaird which, though badly in need of attention, now included a number of valuable coal-mines. Within two years he had married Mary Dundas, a charming girl who was twenty-four years younger than her husband. They had several children, and Bruce, a rich man with a fine house (which he rebuilt), was happy enough dispensing patronage and hospitality. He went through his collections. He indulged his passion for astronomy by erecting an observatory on the top of his house, and there he could often be found dressed in a turban and Ethiopian costume, observing those same stars which had looked down on him so long ago in the Ethiopian mountains. He continued to be an active horseman, but he grew so fat that his carriage was observed to bend sideways when he got into it. He was a laird in the grand manner, still with his eccentricities, and gracefully growing old.

Yet still the sullen indignation burned on. He would not publish. He arranged his journals, he made translations of Ethiopian documents, but resolutely he refused to commit anything to print. It well could have been that things would have gone on like this, but one more tragedy awaited him. In 1788, when he was fifty-eight, his young wife died. Bruce felt this blow very deeply, and in an effort to rouse him from his apathy and melancholy friends urged him to bring out an account of his travels; and at last he gave way. After all, the critics had had their moment of malice fourteen years before and were hardly likely to return to the attack a second time. The book was to be his final justification.

When it appeared in 1790, seventeen years after Bruce's return from Ethiopia, it was a handsome affair of five large quarto volumes entitled *Travels to discover the Sources of the Nile, in the years 1768, 1769, 1770, 1771, 1772, and 1773, by James Bruce of Kinnaird Esq., F.R.S.*, and it was dedicated to George III. In his preface Bruce declares that he will not deign to reply to "any cavills, captious or idle objections" which the critics might raise: "What I have written I have written."

"His enemies," says his biographer, "with pens in their hands, had impatiently waited for his book, like Shylock, whetting his knife, and it was no sooner published, than Bruce was deprived of what was actually nearest to his heart—his honor and his reputation. It was useless to stand against the storm that assailed him; it was impossible to swim against the current that overwhelmed him. His volumes were universally disbelieved. . . ."

Once again the old outcry against such stories as the eating of raw beef cut from living cattle was raised; meticulously, wittily, and maliciously the book was reviled and taken to pieces. Walpole found the five volumes "dull and dear." It seemed that there was no length to which literary London would not go to turn Bruce into a laughing-stock.

Morose and enraged, Bruce retired into his shell in Scotland. Occasionally he made brief visits to London, but he remained for the most part with his family at Kinnaird entertaining his neighbors. The news of the French revolution and of the execution of his old patron Louis XVI increased his disgust with the outside world. Just occasionally he flared up, as when a guest at a country house-party was rash enough to say that it was impossible that the Ethiopians could eat uncooked meat. Bruce went out to the kitchen and returned with a piece of raw beef which he had peppered and salted in the Ethiopian manner. "You will either eat that, sir, or fight me," he said. When the unfortunate guest had consumed the whole steak Bruce said, "Now, sir, you will never again say it is impossible."

The last act was tragic. Bruce had been entertaining a large party at Kinnaird, and having seen off one of his guests, was hurrying up the great staircase of his house to fetch another when he tripped and fell. He pitched onto his head. He lived for a few hours but never regained consciousness. He was just sixty-four.

It is still a little difficult to assess Bruce's place in African travels. Long after his death—for forty years at least—his book was believed by many people to be romantic fiction, and critics continued to attack it. Yet almost from the first it had a popular success, and in the last 150 years it has been repeatedly reprinted and read all over the world. Copies of the first edition, which were once burned as wastepaper in Dublin, are now valuable items in the shops that sell rare books. It is hard to understand why his contemporaries should have failed to see here a work of major originality and importance which stuck to the truth in all its more serious facts, and which was far in advance of the scientific and geographical knowledge of Ethiopia at that time. No one doubted Captain Cook, a contemporary of Bruce's, who brought back accounts of equally marvelous things from the South Pacific. We in our own age may have some reservations about the information given us by the first men who reach the moon, but we are hardly likely to revile them or treat them with contempt. We will think them very brave. Bruce was brave too.

But Bruce's place may be even more complicated than this. He was disbelieved but he was not ignored. He gave life to a legend, he stirred up people's imaginations; at a time when European politics and ambitions were moving outward he turned people's attention to the Nile.

These effects were even more important in France than they were in England, for the French had never scouted Bruce's achievements. They took him very seriously. And so by the end of the eighteenth century an attraction towards Africa was building itself up in France, and it needed only some dominant figure to give it direction and force. Now at last the long Egyptian sleep was ending, and the great eruption into the Nile valley was ready to begin.

CHAPTER FOUR

BONAPARTE SETS OUT

NAPOLEON BONAPARTE'S admiring biographer, Thiers, describes the French invasion of Egypt as "the rashest attempt that history records." But was it really so? In the year 1798 French arms were everywhere victorious; it was really a matter of finding fresh battlefields for the revolutionary army, since it was filled with confidence and eager for more victories.

It was true that England was still in the field, but what could England do? The Royal Navy might be very strong, but its morale had recently been damaged by two mutinies, and for some time past England had withdrawn her fleet from the Mediterranean, merely contenting herself with the blockade of Cadiz. Her best ships were needed nearer at home, since she herself was in imminent danger of invasion, and it was by no means certain that the French army would not manage to get ashore, either in Ireland or in the vicinity of Folkestone, on the south coast. The French, in fact, were actively planning just such an expedition.

Nor was the Egyptian campaign a hastily conceived project or a mere pretext for continuing the war. Bonaparte had been preparing for it for a long time. He had very carefully studied affairs in the Near East,[1] and he had every reason to believe that the Ottoman Empire was far too weak to defend its distant province in Egypt, and that in Egypt itself the Mamelukes, the rulers of Egypt, were a worn-out military clique of medieval backwardness. How could their cavalry hope to contend with

[1] In 1797 Milan's celebrated library was removed by the French as part of their booty. When the books arrived in Paris it was found that nearly every volume relating to the East was annotated by marginal notes in Bonaparte's handwriting.

the new infantry tactics and modern artillery? Bonaparte's friend Volney had traveled widely through the Sultan's dominions, and had provided him with very full information on this score. "The forces of the Mamelukes," Volney had written, "are a rabble, their way of fighting a duel, their war merely brigandage."

As for Alexandria, the port at which presumably the French would land, it was defenseless: "One sees there no fortifications of any kind: the lighthouse, even with its high towers, is no bastion. There are not four cannon in order, and not a single gunner who knows how to aim them. The five hundred Janissaries who are supposed to form the garrison have been reduced in numbers by a half, and are common workmen who hardly know how to light a pipe."

Once conquered, Egypt would not be difficult to govern. "There is no country in the world," Bonaparte was to write later, "where the government controls more closely, by means of the Nile, the life of the people. Under a good administration the Nile gains on the desert: under a bad one, the desert gains on the Nile."

There were visions of glory in all this, dreams of Alexandrian conquests in the fabulous east, but even the most superficial study of Bonaparte's actions at this time shows that he was very far from being carried away by his own enthusiasm. He was very cool and very practical. He was not a Hitler making impassioned speeches; he was a newly arrived young general of incredible confidence, quietly and precisely imposing his will upon the men who held the power in Paris. He had conquered Italy, not to enjoy a popular success, but to prepare himself for the next jump forward.

Now at the age of twenty-eight he was very well aware that he was the idol of all France; indeed, this was made evident to him every day in Paris. The street where he had bought his little house had been renamed Rue de la Victoire, and he could not emerge from it without exuberant crowds pressing around him. He had but to enter a theater for the audience to rise and applaud. But no man ever had fewer delusions about himself than Bonaparte. When his secretary, Bourrienne, remarked upon his popularity one day he replied, "Bah, the crowd would flock to see me just as eagerly if I were going to the scaffold." It was true, of course. It was also true that he could not continue for long as the national hero unless he consolidated his reputation with new victories. The important thing at this stage, however, is that Bonaparte saw all this very clearly—just as clearly as he saw that the Directory, the government of France, feared him and therefore hated him and wanted to get rid of him. He on his side despised the Directors.

And so he affects to fall in with the government's plans. He accepts the command of the expedition to invade England, he even makes a tour of the Channel ports, detaches privateers to reconnoiter the English coast between Rye and Folkestone, and places orders for cannon of an English type that can be loaded with captured ammunition once the French army is ashore.

One cannot say that Bonaparte was absolutely opposed to the direct invasion of England, but it was obvious from the first that he did not like it. It was significant that although the hatred of England in France was very great at this time (the early spring of 1798), a government appeal for a loan of eighty million francs to finance the expedition failed miserably. Now was the moment to maneuver the attention of the Directory away from the English Channel and back to the Mediterranean. Bonaparte declared his plan: "To go to Egypt, to establish myself there and found a French colony, will require some months. But as soon as I have made England tremble for the safety of India, I shall return to Paris, and give the enemy its deathblow. There is nothing to fear in the interval. Europe is calm. Austria cannot move, England is occupied with preparing her defense against invasion, and Turkey will welcome the expulsion of the Mamelukes." Elsewhere he said that if he sailed in May he thought he might be back in October, but he was by no means certain about this. When his wife Josephine later asked him when he would return, he is said to have answered: "Six months, six years, perhaps never." But this reply may perhaps have been induced by the momentary despondency of parting from her;

on all occasions, now and later, Bonaparte had his eye firmly fixed upon France. To the Directory, however, the time element hardly mattered; long or short, the main thing was to get him out of the way, and so by March 1798 we find them coming around to the Egyptian plan.

One pauses here to glance once again at the phenomenon of how the young man had got himself into such a commanding position. Granted that he was a prodigy from birth, granted that the revolution had opened for him opportunities that would never have come his way under Louis XVI, it is still a fact that a bare four years earlier his name was nothing in the world. This was a revolutionary atmosphere when youth was everything and a reputation could be made in a day. Yet he was still a gauche figure in the Parisian salons, long uncombed hair straggling down to his shoulders, a sallow complexion, somber blue eyes, an air of fatigue and dull restlessness, a short, thin, ugly body covered with clothes that were ill-kept and too big for him. His sword draggled ineffectually at his side. Perhaps these outward effects might not have counted for much among intelligent people, but he was generally silent, and when he did speak it was with an ungainly Corsican accent. In brief, he is the intense young genius who is perfectly conscious of his own superior powers and just as perfectly unable to see how he will ever manage to express them.

Now however, in 1798, two tremendous years in Italy had intervened, and General Bonaparte at twenty-eight was an unrecognized genius no longer. His appearance may have been as uncompromising as ever, but now his face has the stamp of a man in authority. He exerts authority as naturally as he breathes.

Desaix, one of his ablest generals, might easily have been jealous of this spectacular rival, for he was a year older than Bonaparte and his career hardly less successful. At the age of twenty-eight he had risen to the command of the army on the Rhine, and he was the prototype of everything a revolutionary general ought to be, an utterly concentrated soldier, full of courage and shrewd decisions, who lived in the field with his men and had no affectations of any kind. It was said that in the thick of a battle Desaix's little figure seemed to increase in height and his voice took on a note of absolute command; and so his troops would follow him anywhere. But Desaix had no thought of making his own independent way in the world. He instantly recognized Bonaparte as his superior, and offered his services. "I am persuaded," he declared about this time, "that Bonaparte will achieve so immense a glory that it is impossible that it will not reflect on his lieutenants. . . . He is proud, hidden, never forgives. He follows his enemy to the end of the world." Not unnaturally the new commander in chief liked Desaix very much.

Bonaparte's influence upon the intellectuals of the Institute of France seems even more remarkable. Success, of course, is infectious, and in every age intellectuals have always been charmed by literate men of action, but Bonaparte appears to have roused the Institute as though it were a corps of cadets about to follow him into battle. They invite him to become a member, and they are delighted by the modest air with which he reads his papers, astonished at his knowledge and flattered by his interest in their work. All at once respectable men of science and letters, men like Monge and Berthollet who are many years his senior, find themselves becoming young again, and they can think of nothing so exciting as to go off on a military expedition to Egypt. The young commander is more than welcoming. He wants them all on his staff, engineers, geologists, mathematicians, chemists, zoologists, astronomers, geographers, mineralogists, archaeologists, arabists, poets and painters; and in the end, almost without realizing what was happening to them, these sedentary and studious men really do become another corps of cadets following young Caesar into battle.

Meanwhile the plans for the campaign went forward with the same sure touch. From the first it was almost a private expedition; once he had got his credit from the Directory (a sum of some nine million francs), Bonaparte rendered no accounts, spent the money as he wished, and it was certainly not the

Ministry of War which was the operational headquarters: it was the little house in the Rue de la Victoire. He absolutely rejected the Directory's demand that they should send commissars on the expedition to watch his movements, and the general outline of the plan seems to have been entirely of his own making. He estimated that he needed a force of something over thirty thousand infantry and three thousand cavalry, supported by a hundred guns. These in the main were to be drawn from the soldiers he had so successfully commanded in Italy, and his generals of brigade and division were to be the men he himself had promoted or appointed: Desaix and Kléber, Berthier, Murat, Marmont, Lannes, Davout and Junot. Josephine's son Eugène de Beauharnais was added to the staff as his aide-de-camp. Most of these men were as young as Bonaparte himself, many had been wounded in his service; and thus they followed him with the spirit that belongs only to young men who have already risked themselves in battle and have survived to enjoy the intoxication of power. This, perhaps more than any other single factor, ensured the success of the expedition.

Next the ships had to be assembled, thirteen sail of the line with their accompanying frigates, and two hundred or more transports for the troops. Toulon was to be the main port of embarkation, and other contingents were to join from Marseilles, Genoa, Corsica and Civitavecchia. Malta was to be the first objective, and once the island was secured the entire fleet was to sail in company for Alexandria.

Bonaparte is said to have feared the sea and to have never understood it. Yet nothing in his career is more astonishing than the speed and precision with which this complicated and dangerous amphibious operation was set up in Paris in a few short months in the spring of 1798. From the Rue de la Victoire a stream of orders go out, and are obeyed with an alacrity that no modern general could ever hope to achieve with all the aids of aircraft, the telegraph and the telephone. It is a conspiracy in the grand manner, and nothing is forgotten. Monge is sent off to obtain maps, and Arabic and Greek printing presses, a library is collected for the expedition, a French soldier who had served against the British in India is enlisted in the intelligence corps, the annual rise and fall of the Nile is studied and it is agreed that the army must arrive in Egypt before the flood begins in August; sappers, miners and a medical staff are appointed, and a letter goes off to Admiral Brueys asking for a berth on a ship "suitable for a commander in chief who expects to be sea-sick the entire voyage."

A fresh wind of hope and excitement blows through all this. It was certainly true that not all the soldiers were eager for the adventure—there were dissensions both in the fleet and the army assembling in Toulon—but nobody seriously questions the plan or raises doubts about the commander in chief. Already Bonaparte's name is a guarantee of success, and this in itself was a remarkable thing, since the soldiers and sailors had no inkling of where they were going or how long they would be away. They were simply told in a vague way that they were to strike a blow against England, and this inevitably meant that many of them would never see their homes again.

One still finds it hard to understand how the secret of the expedition's destination was so well kept; many people knew the plan in Paris, couriers were traveling all over France and Italy, regiments were on the move and the ships assembling in the ports were there for all to see. The British knew well enough that an expedition was being prepared, but the fact remains that long after the French fleet had sailed they still believed that either a descent was to be made on Naples or that Bonaparte, turning west through the Straits of Gibraltar, would head for England or Ireland.

It might also be wondered how Brueys could so confidently set out with his unwieldy convoy of several hundred small transports, knowing that at any moment the British fleet could put in an appearance in the western Mediterranean—indeed, already in early May there were reports of British frigates cruising off Corsica and Toulon. But the sheer size of the Mediterranean was greatly to the French advantage, and these were still the days of sail. It was a full month's voyage from Toulon to Alexandria, and even so large an expedition as this could reasonably hope to conceal its movements in that great expanse of sea. Nor can it be assumed that in 1798 the French acknowledged the superiority of the British fleet. Nelson had still to fight his greatest battles, and the Mediterranean for the French was a familiar sea. They might not have welcomed a conflict when they were impeded by their convoy, but it cannot be asserted that their captains were afraid to fight. Given the right conditions they may even have been eager for a contest; after all, that was what their thirteen ships of the line and their fourteen frigates were designed for.

And so as the day of embarkation drew near there was a growing confidence in the expedition. The size of the force (with the addition of the sailors it now numbered about 40,000) was an assurance in itself, and as usually happens on these occasions both soldiers and sailors took heart from the fact that they together were committed irrevocably to a great adventure.

On May 4, 1798, Bonaparte slipped quietly out of Paris. He traveled with Josephine in the first of two carriages and reached Toulon in the excellent time of five days. The port was alive with the stir and movement of the embarkation, and soldiers were everywhere, the infantry in their black, knee-length gaiters, tight white breeches, coats faced with scarlet, and the revolutionary cockade in their hats, the officers in their shakos and epaulettes. Bonaparte issued the customary exhortation to the troops. They were, he declared, "a wing of the Army of England," and at the successful conclusion of the expedition each man was to be given six acres of land.

By May 12 the embarkation was complete, but a storm had blown up and Brueys waited until May 18 for it to abate. Then at last he gave the word to sail. On May 19 Bonaparte went on board *L'Orient*, a ship of the line with 120 guns, with Berthier and his personal staff, and followed the rest of the fleet out to sea.

Who in this present age can ever hope to know the life and excitement of an armada of sailing ships setting out on an invasion? Through two world wars we have grown used to dark embarkations in the night and the sinister secret shapes of destroyers and submarines, the ominous aircraft overhead. But here it was all bulging canvas, flags flying, the bands playing, the soldiers in bright uniforms on the decks, and the rolling natural movement of the sea. It was a lovely day. The frigates led the way, followed by the ships of the line and then the smaller transports in their scores, bobbing about for miles astern on the bright blue water. Brueys before sailing had received a report that a squadron of thirty British ships had been sighted off Majorca heading northeast, but today the sea was empty, and without incident the fleet sailed on to Genoa and Ajaccio to pick up the reinforcements. Turning east again to the Italian coast they hove to off Civitavecchia, but word was sent out to them from the shore that Desaix, who had been assembling his division there, had sailed a day or two earlier for Malta, and so they went on again. On June 9 they arrived off the island to find that Desaix was already engaged in parleying with the Knights of St. John.

Shafik Ghorbal, the Egyptian historian, recounts that "one day's skirmishes and another of negotiations sufficed to bring about the fall of Malta," and the event really does appear to have happened as simply as this: the garrison collapsed under the first assault.

On June 19, the commander in chief was ready to sail again. There was still no sign of the English, and the French fleet, now swollen to over 300 vessels, headed east in perfect weather with a following northwest breeze.

Twelve days' sailing lay before them, and it appears to have been a pleasant voyage; not even Bonaparte was sea sick. He spent his days aboard *L'Orient* dictating to Bourrienne, reading a good deal from the 287 improving books in the expedition's library, and watching comedies improvised by the soldiers and the crew. The soldiers were kept active by climbing the masts and by daily gun drill, and there were frequent alerts to prepare them for the appearance of the English ships. But still the English did not come, and for the moment, on this calm summer sea, the expedition was locked away entirely from the world.

At this stage Bonaparte may really have deluded himself

briefly that he might be accepted by the Egyptians as one of themselves. At all events this was the public role he designed for himself at this critical moment of landing, and he put the matter very forcibly to his own troops. No mosques were to be violated, no Moslem priests were to be disturbed, no plunder was to be taken, and no woman was to be molested—the Frenchman who did that was a scoundrel. In every unit officers were instructed to enforce the strictest discipline in the soldiers' treatment of the civilians. As they came up to the Egyptian coast many of the men may have wondered just what rewards they *were* to have in this distant eldorado. "There you are," cried some wit, pointing to the flat and gloomy shoreline. "There are the six acres that have been promised you."

Up to this point—it was now July 1—Bonaparte had been exceptionally lucky. For the past six weeks Nelson with fourteen ships had been fruitlessly chasing him up and down the Mediterranean, and had in fact called in at Alexandria only two days before. Finding no sign of the French the British had sailed away again at the very moment when the leading French frigates were approaching the coast. It had been Bonaparte's original intention to sail directly into Alexandria harbor and, if possible, take the town by surprise. But now word reached him that the Egyptian garrison was already forewarned, and thus the landing would have to be made on the open beaches to the west of the city. This was a serious setback, since a storm had blown up and heavy waves were breaking on the shore.

Bonaparte gave orders for disembarkation. Dispositions were made to bring the convoy as near to land as the danger of running ashore, during a high wind, would permit. The ships of war formed an outer circle of defense. All their sails were furled and their anchors cast.

But still the sea continued to rise, and all day went by before the first troops were got ashore.

"The boats," wrote an onlooker, "received one by one and at random the soldiers descending from the vessels; when they were filled the waves appeared every instant to be on the point of swallowing them; or, at the mercy of the wind, they were forced upon others; and after escaping all this, on gaining the shore, they knew not where to touch without bilging on the breakers." And so things continued through the night.

Bonaparte himself got ashore shortly before midnight, and he slept briefly on the sand among the soldiers. At dawn he rose and immediately took command of the four-thousand-odd men who had struggled onto the beach. A small Bedouin fort named Marabu was assaulted and taken. Four miles away across the desert the French could see the walls and minarets of Alexandria. Forming his men into three columns, one heading for Pompey's Pillar, another for the catacombs, and the third for the Rosetta Gate, Bonaparte led the way on foot across the sand.

CHAPTER FIVE

EGYPT AND THE MAMELUKES

EGYPT was not easy to defend. The great deserts to the west of the Nile offered a formidable barrier, and no one attempted to penetrate the country that way,[1] but a landing could be made at any place on the low flat shoreline of the delta, and there was a safe anchorage at Alexandria. Once Alexandria fell and the Rosetta mouth of the Nile was taken, no mountains impeded the advance of the invader inland, and he was certain to find food and water nearly all the way to Cairo, over one hundred miles to the south.

The delta was a great prize. Here in this artificial garden where rain hardly ever fell but where fresh water was plentiful, two or even three crops were gathered every year, and the annual flooding of the Nile provided a rich layer of silt several inches deep. With comparatively little labor every good thing in life sprang up in abundance, rice and sugar-cane, coffee and tobacco, cotton and flax, lentils and dates, flowers and vines. So long as the water was distributed through the flat land by canals there was no limit to this fertility. Frosts and storms were almost unknown, and most plagues and pests succumbed eventually in the dry antiseptic air of the desert. Except for occasional sandstorms and a muggy, soporific quality in the air during the floods in September, the heat was not excessive, and the winter months were very nearly perfect.

At the time of Bonaparte's landing the population of Egypt was about two and a half million, which was a third of what it was estimated to have been in the days of the Pharaohs and

[1] It was tried by the mechanized forces of the Germans and Italians in the Second World War and they failed.

hardly more than a tenth of what it is at present. The people were a mixed lot. Far away in Upper Egypt the Nubian tribes clung to their strips of vegetation along the river bank and in the cultivated oases. Provincial governors sent out from Cairo gathered taxes from them and maintained a rough and ready sort of administration, but for the most part life went by on the Upper Nile in ignorance and solitude. The Bedouin who roamed the intervening deserts that formed fourteen-fifteenths of Egypt were also very largely a law unto themselves, and cannot have numbered more than a few tens of thousands. By far the largest part of the population was huddled into the delta. Apart from the Mamelukes, whom we must consider in a moment, the delta population consisted of about 1,750,000 fellaheen, the natives who cultivated the soil and formed the laboring population of the cities; about 150,000 Copts—Egyptians who worshiped Christ and fulfilled more or less the role of money-lenders, traders and government officials—and finally the foreigners. These last numbered perhaps 200,000 and lived almost entirely in the cities. They included Turks (the great majority), Greeks, Armenians, Jews, Syrians and a handful of French traders who, at the first news of Bonaparte's landing, were interned.

The only two cities of any consequence were Cairo and Alexandria, and Alexandria at this time had sunk to the nadir of its fortunes. Of its ancient glory—of its reputed 4,000 palaces, its theaters, temples and monuments that had once made it second only to Rome in the Roman Empire—hardly anything remained. Pompey's Pillar still stood, and the walls still rose to a height of forty feet in some places, but for the rest all had sunk into dust and rubble, the canal from the Nile had silted up, and the inhabitants, decimated by repeated plagues, had dwindled to less than 10,000. An observer who got into the city on the heels of the French assault says he found the houses shut up, the streets deserted except for a few ragged women trailing about like ghosts among the ruins, and a universal silence broken only by the cries of the kites. Even Pompey's Pillar seen from close to was not very impressive.

Cairo, on the other hand, was a flourishing place; after

Constantinople it was the most important city in the Near East, with a population of about 250,000 people. Since it was first founded over a thousand years before it had been rebuilt several times, and the present city (variously known as Masr, Misr, El-Kahira or Grand Cairo) stood on the site of an ancient Roman fortress. It lay a little distance from the right bank of the river under the cover of the Mokattam Hills, and was ringed by high walls and dominated by a citadel.

The skyline, seen from a distance, had romantic aspects: the domes and minarets of 300 mosques rose from the smoke of cooking fires, and the palm trees and cultivated fields along the river bank gave the place a placid and rather rural air. The citadel, built by Saladin in the twelfth century, was a fine complex of dun-colored battlements, and in the desert beyond, on the opposite side of the river, one descried the pyramids. Seen from closer at hand, however, these noble prospects disintegrated. Except for the large open squares such as the Esbekiah, which were flooded and thronged with boats during the annual inundation of the Nile, the city was a warren of narrow unpaved streets and nondescript Turkish houses covering about three square miles. Rubbish lay about on every side, the haunt of scavenging dogs and cats, and in the worst slums it was hard to say which were the ruins of fallen buildings and which the hovels of the present generation.

Yet no one with any love for oriental life could resist this place. The day began before dawn when the muezzins (many of them chosen because they were blind and thus unable to see down into the private houses) roused the people with their first call to the mosques: "Come to prayer. Come to security. God is most great." Within an hour—that first fresh hour of the Egyptian morning—the life of the city spilled itself out into the streets, the bazaars and the coffee-houses, and at every turn the passer-by was bound to come on a spectacle of some kind: a marriage or a funeral, an impromptu performance of strolling players in the square, a well-to-do merchant trotting along on his ass with a slave running in front to clear the way, a string of camels thrusting through the crowds with their heads held high and disdainfully in the air. There was a constant passage of street-vendors shouting up to the balconies overhead, and of water-carriers with goat-skins slung round their shoulders, and a hullabaloo of shouts and cries filled the air: "*Ya bint; dahrak,*" "Watch thy back, daughter," "*Ya efendee,*" "Take care," "O consoler of the embarrassed, my supper must be thy gift"—this last from the innumerable beggars whom one refused by replying with some such phrase as "God will sustain."

Craftsmen did their work in their shops under the customer's eye; there was one street for gold- and silversmiths and jewelers, another for leatherworkers and brass-founders, others for potters, silk-spinners, makers of weapons, dyers and perfumers.

Nightfall and darkness (there were no street lights) put an end to the hubbub. Soon after the muezzins' fifth and final call the gates of the city were locked, and many of the streets with large wooden doors at either end were shut up for the night as well. "One might pass through the whole length of the metropolis," a writer says, "and scarcely meet more than a dozen or twenty persons, excepting the watchmen and guards, and the porters at the gates of the bystreets and quarters. The sentinel, or guard, calls out to the approaching passenger in Turkish, 'Who is that?' and is answered in Arabic, 'A citizen.' The private watchman, in the same case, exclaims, 'Attest the unity of God!' or merely, 'Attest the unity!' The reply given to this is, 'There is no deity but God!' "

The Nile was the all-provider of this existence. It grew every ounce of food, it supplied water to the wells which were dug in each quarter of the city, and it was the main highway to the outside world. The ceremony of the opening of the canals when the flood rose in August was one of the great occasions of the year. The river at Cairo was about half a mile wide, but it was divided by two islands, Bulaq and Rhoda, where crops were grown and where some of the wealthier people had their pleasure-gardens. Memphis, the ancient capital a little further up the river, had decayed to nothing. In the desert at Gizeh the Sphinx lay buried up to its neck in sand, its nose already broken.

There was one other aspect of the city which gave it a special importance, and which made travelers think of it not simply as Cairo but Grand Cairo: it was the great terminal of the caravan routes that spread out over northern Africa and the Near East. No one dreamed of traveling alone through the desert any more than one would dream of crossing the Atlantic in a canoe. You waited until a caravan was being formed in Cairo, and then applied to the sheikh in command for permission to accompany it. Sometimes months would go by before all was ready, and then on a certain day the order to march would be given, and a long straggling procession of camels, mules, donkeys, and men on foot would set off into the desert. Incoming caravans signaled their arrival at the pyramids and were then told where to cross the Nile and encamp. The distances covered were prodigious. One route—and of course there were no clearly defined tracks in the desert, merely a general line of march that led on from one water-hole or oasis to the next—took you northeast to Damascus where the traveler could join other caravans headed for Aleppo and Baghdad; another carried the pilgrims down to Mecca and the Red Sea; another followed the general course of the Nile to Sennar and Darfur in the Sudan; still another led off to Fezzan in the west. Every journey was an adventure, and the traders, like migratory birds, were controlled by the seasons and beset at every stage by unpredictable hazards such as civil wars, Bedouin raids, drought, floods and sickness. A year, two years on the road—this was nothing to an experienced merchant. Taking with him his wives, his children and his slaves, he would go on and on wherever the markets offered a profit, and in the end nomadism became an object in itself, and many of these men could endure no other way of life. No one knew the extent of this vast, haphazard network. It was quite possible for a man to travel from Egypt to Timbuktu on the other side of Africa, and it is certain that Indian and even Chinese goods appeared in the bazaars in Cairo.

The merchants dealt in kind rather than in money. In Cairo they obtained grain, rice, cotton, flax, and the thousand and one products of the bazaars. These things, increasing in value with every mile they traveled, would be bartered for other goods in the Near East and in the primitive villages in the far interior of Africa. The Sudan trade was particularly profitable. It produced black slaves, gold, ivory, ostrich feathers, rhinoceros horn, gum arabic, ebony, coffee (brought from Ethiopia) and spices (from the Red Sea). Petroleum was also brought in small quantities from the Arabian Gulf; it was either drunk as a medicine or rubbed on the body. Thus there was a continual interchange at Cairo, a constant ebb and flow of strange faces and of strange goods displayed for sale, a commotion of arrivals and departures.

In our time a thousand travelers' books and a spate of illustrated magazines and moving pictures have made a cliché of the East, but in 1798 nothing in Egypt was familiar to the Europeans. Travelers marveled at everything they saw, and what they did not understand they tended to dismiss as decadent, superstitious and uncouth. It seemed ridiculous, for example, that the Egyptians, on the occasion of a death in the family, should turn their furniture upside down; and that they should believe that, with music, they could charm snakes out of their houses. The music itself was just a noise to European ears, and the Moslem prayers a groveling on the ground. The sheikh, sitting cross-legged by the hour on his divan, appeared to be merely apathetic and dull.

Yet the Egyptians were not quite so decadent as the West has liked to imagine, either before or since. The sheikhs were very far from being apathetic and dull: they were the men of law and religion in the community and they were greatly respected. The Koran which they expounded put the strongest strictures upon everybody's life, and in the main they were obeyed. The seven deadly sins in Egypt are very interesting: disobedience to parents, murder, desertion during an expedition against infidels, usury, falsely accusing a woman of adultery, idolatry and the wasting of the property of orphans.

It would be absurd, of course, to make out that the Egyptians were paragons of virtue compared, say, with the invading French—they lied, they stole, they were superstitiously ignorant, they were always lazy when they had the chance, and were probably cowards as well, but they also had a certain dignity in their lives, they knew patience and quietude (which the French did not), and they were graceful, even beautiful, people.

They lived in a kind of torpor and they had no will for change. The Muhammadan religion, with its absolute rules, suited them perfectly and they never dreamed of questioning it. They never even thought of revolting against their rulers, the Mamelukes.

The Egyptian priests and sheikhs who were confused about so much else were not taken in for two minutes by Bonaparte's declaration that he had come to rescue them from the Mamelukes. They knew that he wanted the power for himself and (unlike the Mamelukes) they suspected that it was useless to resist him.

The Mamelukes themselves were hardly less conservative than their subjects; a stranger group of men it is hardly possible to conceive.

The word Mameluke means male slave, more especially a white male slave, but they were slaves of a special kind. They were purchased as children from poor peasant families in Georgia and the Caucasus, and then imported into Egypt, where they were brought up by their masters (who had also been slaves in their time) with the express purpose of ruling the country. War was the Mamelukes' trade. From their earliest years they were trained as horsemen and warriors. Through the years they had steadily increased in numbers; the total Mameluke population with its dependants in 1798 numbered nearly 100,000. The great majority of them lived in Cairo.

These supermen saw to it that they looked and behaved like supermen. Many of them were tall and strikingly handsome, and their costume was a wonder to behold: a green cap wreathed with a large yellow turban, a coat of chain mail beneath a long robe that was bound at the waist by an embroidered shawl, voluminous red pantaloons, leather gauntlets, and red, pointed slippers. Each man's armament consisted of a brace of pistols, a mace, a long curved sword, a sheaf of arrows, and an English carbine, all with handles and blades chased in silver and copper designs of fine workmanship and sometimes studded with precious stones. Thus encumbered they were mounted upon an enormous saddle of wood and iron—each of the copper stirrups alone weighed thirteen pounds—and it was nothing for a man to pay the equivalent of over a thousand dollars for a mount. Their horses were the finest Arabs, and probably as cavalry the Mamelukes had no equal in the world; they charged with utter recklessness and fought with a ferocity that was a byword in the East. "They start," says one observer, "like lightning and arrive like thunder." Once unhorsed, however, they were heavily encumbered by their arms, and it was left to their irregular Bedouin infantry to save the day.

The Ibn Tulun mosque in Cairo, the first pure mosque to be built in the world, and possibly the most beautiful building in Africa, was the work of a Mameluke. The huge domed and minareted tombs of the Mameluke beys, standing in the desert outside the walls of Cairo, are also an architectural triumph of their kind, and not even the dust and squalor of the slums that now surround them, or the hordes of ragged children who haunt this city of the dead, can quite obscure the revelation that there was a vision here that rose above a barbarous and material life.

As for the houses which the Mamelukes inhabited within the city walls, they were rather disappointing on the outside: rickety-looking structures of wood and stone with balconies that projected so far they almost formed a roof over the narrow streets below. But inside their houses the wealthier men indulged themselves in great splendor: a fountain playing in the courtyard fell into a pool lined with black and white marble, mosaics and wooden lattice-work decorated the walls, and Persian carpets were spread upon the floor. In place of chairs there were divans with silken cushions and coverings. No room, not even the harem upstairs, was specifically designed as a bedroom—the bedding was put away in a cupboard by day and laid out at any convenient place at night; very often, in hot weather, one slept on the roof. The general object inside the house was to exclude the hot sunlight, and thus the Mameluke sat with his friends in a fine cool gloom eating his three daily meals (one before dawn, another at 10 a.m. and a third at 5 p.m.), sipping his coffee and sherbet, or puffing at the carved and jeweled ivory mouthpiece of his water-pipe while, sometimes, he watched a performance of musicians and dancers. Needless to say, their retinues of slaves were very large: one man to guard the door, another to carry water, a third to run before his master and clear a way through the crowded streets, and many others to staff the house. The establishments of the more powerful men were tremendous; it was nothing for a bey to have several hundred Circassian slaves, all armed and mounted, and each of these slaves would be attended by two or three Egyptian servants of his own.

Their wealth came mostly from customs dues. The merchant caravans that picked up goods from the Red Sea ships and transported them to the Mediterranean were charged enormous sums. Twenty-eight thousand dollars worth of Indian spices would pay up to $25,000 on the passage through Egypt (which was one reason why the British had developed the trade round the Cape of Good Hope), and the desert caravans were taxed as well. Upon the income from this trade, as well as upon plunder and the ruthless exploitation of the Egyptians, the Mamelukes lived the full, rich life.

To rule, if not by the sword, then by bribery and treachery—this was the mainspring of their existence. And despite murderous quarrels among themselves, endless intrigues and a morality that made a virtue of broken faith, they had succeeded in ruling for something over 500 years at the time of Bonaparte's arrival. Generation after generation of Egyptians had succumbed to these gorgeous butchers, and between pogroms, invasions and civil wars, the fellaheen tried to eke out some sort of living by remaining inconspicuous and servile. In short, the Mamelukes lorded it over the land very much as the Pharaohs had in ancient times.

In theory the Mamelukes were still subject to the Sultan in Constantinople; they were bound to pay him an annual bounty and to accept a Viceroy appointed by the Porte. In fact, it was many years since the bounty had been paid, and the present

Viceroy, Abu Bekir Pasha, was hardly more than a puppet of the twenty-three Mameluke beys who composed the government. In recent years two of these beys, Ibrahim and Murad, had formed an uneasy and mutually suspicious partnership in Cairo, and it was they who exercised the real power. In 1798 Ibrahim, a tall, thin figure with an aquiline nose and a reputation for meanness, had reached his sixties, and Murad, the man with whom we are chiefly concerned, was gaining the ascendancy. Murad Bey could neither read nor write; the engravings made of him at the time reveal a patriarchal figure, rather plump, his face wreathed with a fringe of beard, and he sits complacently on his divan smoking his pipe. Nothing could less reveal the real nature of this formidable man. He was in his late forties at this time, and his life had been one long struggle for power. Eight years before, when he had seemed at the summit of success, a Turkish army had landed and driven him into Upper Egypt. But he had returned and had been reinstated, and had married a woman named Fatima who was older than himself (she was about fifty), and the daughter of Ali Bey, the leading Mameluke of the previous reign. She had great wealth, intelligence and influence—all very valuable attributes for a man who was by nature an impetuous and ambitious soldier, an adventurer who was physically tough and energetic even by the standards of the Mamelukes. Murad Bey had a flotilla of boats on the Nile, a pleasure-garden at Gizeh close to the pyramids, and a personal bodyguard of about 400 men. It was accepted that in a crisis he was the general who would lead the Mamelukes into battle, and at this moment very few of his followers doubted that he would succeed.

He felt strong. With his ten thousand cavalry and his thirty thousand irregular infantry he believed that he was more than equal to any invasion of "Franks," however numerous they might be. We are told by a Turkish observer that when the news of the landing first reached Murad in Cairo "his eyes became red and fire devoured his entrails." He summoned Carlo Rossetti, the Venetian consul, and sounded him out about the French. It was in vain that Rossetti tried to make Murad realize who

Bonaparte was, and to explain the power of modern arms. Murad ridiculed the French, calling them "donkey-boys" whom he did not wish to hurt; they should be given a present and sent away; it was absurd to think that they might conquer Egypt.

And so one finds here all the makings of a major tragedy, a genuine clash of ignorant armies. Cut off from the mainstream of Mediterranean civilization for a thousand years or more, caught up in the long, slow cycle of Muhammadan life that turned over and over on itself, advancing nowhere, permitting no new ideas, Egypt was absolutely unprepared for the shock of the French landing. She had no means of knowing that this invasion was quite unlike any other invasion of the past, that it meant the collapse at last of the Middle Ages in the Near East —in Ghorbal's phrase, "the ending of the long Egyptian night."

And the French on their side had their delusions too, for they had no knowledge of campaigning in the desert, no hope of maintaining their conquest without command of the sea, and no real prospect of consolidating their rule in a country that was hostile to nearly everything they stood for. Once the first devastating clash was over the best that could be hoped for was that each side would learn something from the other, that a bridge of a sort would be established between the East and the West, and that then the French would be willing to depart.

Ibrahim, the older and wiser man of the two reigning beys, may have had an inkling of all this, for he is said to have demurred when resistance was proposed during the Mameluke council of war in Cairo. But he was overruled. The army was called out, and Murad himself rode north, at the head of some four thousand cavalry, to meet the invader on the coast.

CHAPTER SIX

THE MARCH TO CAIRO

THE capture of Alexandria proved exceptionally easy. For a few hours the defenders put up a fight from the city walls, but this was merely an outlying garrison, manned by Arabs and Turkish mercenaries rather than by Mamelukes, and they had no real will to struggle with out-of-date cannon in a hopeless cause. Kléber was hit in the forehead by a fragment during the assault, but there were hardly 200 French casualties in all, and after a brief parley Bonaparte set up his headquarters in the center of the town. Here he received the submission of Sheikh Coraim and the other garrison leaders, assuring them that there was to be no vengeance, no tribute, no interference with the local population; they had been liberated, not conquered. On a rapid tour round the town on July 3 Bonaparte ordered the defenses to be put in order, and a French garrison under the command of Menou settled into billets around the walls. Soon the transports of the fleet were sailing in to discharge their stores and the remainder of the soldiers. The ships of the line, uncertain as yet of the depth of the water at the entrance to the harbor, waited in the roadstead outside. Already the printing press, on being landed from *L'Orient*, was striking off copies of Bonaparte's manifesto in Arabic, the first printing ever known in Egypt.

Malta and now Alexandria had fallen at a single blow, and still more important the entire French army, the 30,000 men with a good deal of their equipment, were safely ashore in Egypt. It was a marvelous beginning, and Bonaparte's next move lay clear before him; he must march inland before the Mamelukes had time to realize what he was doing, he must seize the Rosetta mouth of the Nile, and then advance up the river with all possible speed to Cairo.

Two columns were organized; one under Desaix was to march directly towards the Nile and cut it at a place called El Rahmaniya about forty miles from the sea, and the other, commanded by Dugua and accompanied by a flotilla of small boats laden with rice and grain, was to move around the coast to Rosetta. Once the mouth of the Nile was forced the flotilla was to sail upstream and make contact with Desaix at Rahmaniya; the combined army would then advance upon the capital less than one hundred miles away. The men had scarcely time even to see Alexandria, or to accustom their sea legs to the land, before they were marched away into the desert.

Desaix, with his larger column, had some fifty miles to go before he reached the Nile, and these fifty miles were to reveal to the French as nothing else could, and with brutal suddenness, the real nature of the campaign in which they were now involved. At this time the green fields of the delta did not reach anywhere near Alexandria. The canal linking the city with the Nile had long since filled with sand, and the route (which roughly followed the line of the present railway) provided little food or water. It was now midsummer, and the heat was appalling. Dressed in their thick serge coats, breeches and gaiters, laden with their rifles and packs, the men marched in dense columns over heavy sand and rock, kicking up dust as they went along, and there was no shade anywhere. They carried with them a four-day ration of biscuit, but this was not the ideal food to keep thirst at bay, and at the few meager wells along the way water was doled out as though it was the most precious wine. At the end of the first day men were beginning to fall out with blistered feet, sore eyes, and general exhaustion. But they could not fall out. They were being harassed front and rear by Bedouin tribesmen, and no straggler could hope to rest for ten minutes on the sand without being cut off and attacked. Desaix himself was nearly taken when he was hardly fifty yards from the column, and another officer, we learn, was assassinated 100 paces from the advance guard "in consequence of having failed to pay attention, through a melancholic abstraction of mind, to an invitation to keep up with the rest."

In a stupor of fatigue the column struggled on, finding every village in its path deserted and empty of food. Occasionally in the oases there were a few watermelons upon which the soldiers fell like wolves, but that was all. On July 9, after a three days' forced march, they reached Rahmaniya and without waiting to take off their uniforms they threw themselves into the Nile.

And now, suddenly, when the French ranks were in disorder and the men could think of nothing but resting and getting cool, Murad appeared. He had made an excellent march down from Cairo with his cavalry, and they had been accompanied by a flotilla of armed feluccas on the river. Couriers had kept him well posted about the French advance, and now he was ready for battle. With some 800 picked men he came forward along the river bank and stood for a few minutes to survey the French column. It was one of those moments which are the most dramatic if not the most critical in all campaigns, especially in so bizarre a campaign as this: the moment of first contact when both sides are dealing largely in myths and doubts—the myth of the strange enemy before them and the inward inevitable doubt about his own courage that besets every soldier facing the unknown for the first time.

Having by now been a week or more in Egypt the French had heard many stories of the magnificence and the ferocity of the Mamelukes. There was already a rumor in the ranks that Murad led his men into battle mounted on a milk-white camel, his equipment ablaze with gold and precious stones, and that he offered no quarter to his enemies. And so Desaix's weary men were expecting something rather grand and frightening.

The Mamelukes too were quite unprepared for this first shock of recognition, since these Frenchmen were unlike any soldiers they had ever seen before. They regarded them as Bonaparte's slaves, and at this first brief glimpse they thought them very poorly uniformed and probably badly equipped as well, though as yet they could not be absolutely sure about this. Thus no one really knew what was going to happen, fear had a place in everybody's mind, and in their uncertainty both sides set about doing what they had been trained to do; Desaix got his artillery into position and formed his infantry into squares, the first ranks kneeling with the bayonets pointing outwards, the second preparing to fire over their shoulders. The Mamelukes charged.

It was all over in a few minutes. Under the blast of the first cannonade the Mamelukes faltered and wheeled aside into the empty desert. Those who did get near the French squares came under the concentrated fire of the muskets and soon turned back, leaving some forty dead and wounded on the field. Only a dozen of the French were hurt. Bonaparte, coming up to the front with reinforcements, found there was no need for his assistance and having posted his pickets, gave orders for the column to halt for forty-six hours' rest. Neither on the next day nor the day following was there any sign of the Mamelukes returning to the attack. The desert seemed to have swallowed them completely.

Meanwhile Dugua had forced the mouth of the Nile. There had been a tense moment while he got his flotilla of gunboats over the sand-bars there—a high wind was blowing and the river was low—but Rosetta had collapsed without a struggle. Rosetta itself the French found to be "the freshest and most verdant of countries," a garden of dates, bananas, and sycamores among broken and decaying walls. Dugua had at once pressed on, his soldiers marching on the west bank and keeping pace with the boats on the river, and now he had come up to Rahmaniya to join Desaix's column. The plan was working to perfection.

It was now July 12 and Bonaparte was eager to continue the advance, but at dawn the following morning his scouts brought him word that the Mamelukes were standing to meet him in much greater force than before at the village of Jibbrish, a few miles further upstream. Murad, it seemed, had assembled from 3,000 to 4,000 cavalry with which he proposed to block the French approach to the village, while on the Nile itself nine or ten large gunboats were waiting to give battle to the French flotilla.

The French were not quite ready for the encounter—the soldiers were still suffering from fatigue and only 200 of their cavalry were fit for action—but Bonaparte decided to attack at once. He gave orders for his flotilla to sail upstream and thus protect his left flank, while the infantry marched upon Jibbrish, and both were to strike together. He had not, however, calculated the effect of the high north wind; his flotilla was soon driven a good three miles ahead of the army and the French sailors suddenly found themselves confronted with a heavy cannonade both from the banks and the enemy gunboats. In the running battle that followed on the river things went very badly for the French at first: Perrée, their commander, was wounded, and four of their vessels were boarded and seized at the first assault. Hearing the commotion—and something like 1,500 cannon shots were exchanged—Bonaparte hurried his soldiers forward, and they had scarcely time to form their line before the Mamelukes came careering down upon them. Once again the enemy charged directly into the artillery fire, seeking to make a breach in the French squares, at first in front, and then on the flanks, and they came on "like madmen." Those who did succeed in reaching the French infantry hacked away briefly with their sabers until they were killed, but the majority in the vanguard were unhorsed or scattered before they could strike a blow. A second and a third charge brought the same result, and in the early afternoon the Mamelukes finally drew off in a dazed and helpless confusion. They had lost about 300 of their number, and the French soldiers were soon running about looting the bodies. Bonaparte's casualties were barely seventy. Soon too better news arrived from the river; the French had recovered their lost vessels and an explosion on board the principal Mameluke gunboat had been the signal for a general enemy retreat.

In contemporary accounts not a great deal has been made of these two brief engagements on the Lower Nile, and historians have concentrated upon the more imposing battle which was soon to follow outside Cairo. Yet in fact the issue was already decided here on July 13. Up to this point all Bonaparte's careful planning had been hardly more than intelligent conjecture. Wars in the main start with textbooks. But there were no textbooks here, no European army had campaigned in Egypt since the Crusades, no one could speak with finality about the effects of a Mameluke charge, no one knew what unexpected tactics the enemy might produce. But now, in an instant, a gap in history was closed, and the Mamelukes were revealed as expert horsemen who were both incredibly brave and incredibly out of date. It was their misfortune, of course, in this first contact with the West, that they should have to meet the greatest soldier of the age, but even without Bonaparte the French could hardly have failed to demolish so primitive an enemy. In every department of war, in arms, in training and in organization, they were so immeasurably superior as almost to appear as supernatural beings. To the Mamelukes, war was a matter of personal courage, and there was a certain ferocious chivalry about the headlong charge; you triumphed or you died. Everything depended upon speed and movement, the quick tumultuous clash and the breaking away. But this ruthless machine-like French army obeyed none of the accepted rules, it struck from a distance, its tactics were stationary, and its soldiers fought, not as individuals, but as part of the living fortresses they formed on the battlefield. They overturned entirely the medieval notion that cavalry was always superior to infantry, and war was revealed now to the Mamelukes as anything but a hot-blooded skirmish; it was a calculated plan of mass destruction carried out mainly through intense rifle fire and cannon-balls. The charge instead of being the whole battle was merely a secondary affair.

It was true that Murad did not recognize defeat as yet—his main forces were still waiting to give battle outside Cairo—but it was the French who were now the supermen in Egypt, and the Mamelukes could only fight them out of a sense of blind pride, out of desperation and hatred; they could not hope to win.

After the Jibbrish encounter Murad retreated directly to Cairo, eighty miles away, and probably that was the best thing he could have done, since he thus lengthened Bonaparte's line of communication with Alexandria, and the country itself was a far more formidable obstacle to the French than anything the Mamelukes could contrive. The heat grew worse as the soldiers moved inland, and although they often camped among wheat-fields they had no means of making flour. What they craved was bread and wine; what they got was watermelons and lentils, and it was a dangerous diet because the soldiers soon began to complain that they were suffering from dysentery, and dysentery on an empty stomach is a debilitating thing, as every foreign army that has invaded Egypt can testify. Even bathing in the Nile was dangerous. The men were already beginning to feel a painful inflammation of the eyes. Later on this would develop into temporary blindness, and there were other maladies as well—bilharzia and the plague, for example—lying in wait. The French doctors knew very little about these Eastern diseases.

Now too the Bedouin began to harass the column in earnest. These tribesmen were a wholly unexpected hazard, since they constituted a kind of third force in Egypt. They had no common cause with the Mamelukes; it was simply in the nature of their grinding life in the desert to fall on any defenseless traveler who came their way, and every invasion or civil war was the signal for them to take to arms. They pillaged and attacked both sides impartially. They could do no real damage, but like gnats that set upon an elephant they could make life miserable for the French, and it was impossible to come to terms with them.

It was hard for the invaders to know where they were in this strange unrelenting world which was so utterly different from everything that they had been told to expect when they left France. There was no wine, no eatable food, no women, no loot, simply this endless march in battle-order under a blazing sun.

Desaix, moving forward in the van, soon found there was talk of mutiny in his division, and the officers were even louder in complaint than the men. They had not come here, they declared, to die like animals of want, they were hungry, they were tired, they were ill, they could not go on. By the third week of July, when the march had been going on for ten days or more, everyone, men and officers alike, was looking for scapegoats as an outlet for his grievances. One soldier was bold enough to attempt irony with Bonaparte himself: "Well, General, are you going to take us on to India too?" Bonaparte is said to have answered coldly: "No, it's not with men like you that I would undertake that journey."

It was probably the very fact that they *had* to go on that kept the march intact, for by now they had lost all contact with the coast and the French fleet, their one lifeline to France. It was even a retreat of a kind: a retreat to victory.

Had the French known what was happening in Cairo they would have felt a good deal more cheerful. The city was demoralized by the news of Murad's defeat at Jibbrish. He had set out so confidently with his cavalry and his gunboats, and now in a matter of a few days he was back in Cairo, routed and defeated, with this new and terrible French army apparently following on his heels, getting nearer every day.

The first reaction followed the familiar pattern of civilian panic: the run on the food shops, the hiding of valuables and jewels, the preparations for flight. The price of mules and camels rose sharply, weapons of every kind were sold at a premium, and powder and lead became unobtainable in the bazaar. One after another the shops closed their doors and no one stirred in the streets by night. As in every such crisis, when there are signs of fear among those in authority, the lowest people in the community came out into the open. Thieves broke into the houses whose owners had already fled, and mobs set upon the homes of the European merchants and the Copt and Greek churches, ransacking them for jewels and arms. It soon became dangerous for a man to appear alone in a deserted street.

The Mamelukes were able to put a check on some of these excesses. Householders were ordered to hang lanterns from their balconies to light the streets at night when thieves were particularly active, and the people who were attempting flight were arrested at the city gates and imprisoned. Ibrahim called a council of war, and couriers were sent off to the Sultan at Constantinople asking for help—a futile gesture since the French were bound to arrive long before the Sultan could move—but no doubt it created a kind of official reassurance. Meanwhile there was a rough and ready attempt to put Cairo into a state of defence: guns were mounted on the walls and a line of boats was sunk across the Nile near Bulaq to prevent the approach of the French flotilla. A tented camp was set up on the west bank of the river around the village of Embaba, and all men of military age were ordered to assemble there.

These preparations did something to calm the population, but the majority of people preferred to put their trust in God. Prayers were said constantly in the mosques, and the great flag of the Prophet was taken down from the citadel and carried in procession with a band of drums and clarinets to the island of Bulaq, where it was thought the French would first appear. But no one knew precisely what the French were going to do. Would they approach on the west or the east bank, or on the river itself? Each day the bazaars filled with fresh rumors, and Murad's return contributed very little to the general knowledge, since after Jibbrish he had broken off contact with Bonaparte entirely. And now it was decided to adopt a plan which was the last extreme of foolishness: Ibrahim was to remain on the east bank with the reserves covering Cairo, while the main bulk of the Mameluke army under Murad was to take up position in the desert at Embaba on the west bank. Thus Bonaparte, who was already on the west side of the Nile, was to be spared the danger and difficulty of crossing the river before the battle was joined.

A general move was now made to Embaba, and traders and food merchants set up their booths there among the troops. Guns taken from the river-boats were placed around the camp, and the digging of a rough system of trenches was begun. By July 20 some sixty thousand men were assembled, but of these only the Mameluke cavalry, numbering about ten thousand, could be described as an organized force: the remainder were infantry and camp followers, many of whom were armed only with spears and swords. In Cairo women and children and aged people who had been left behind remained hidden in their houses.

Bonaparte during these eventful days steadily continued his advance up the river. "Melancholy and sadness," he records, "reigned in the army." But still he pushed his murmuring soldiers on, and ate his own plate of lentils in the midst of their bivouacs at night.

On July 19 they reached Umm Dinar, close to the junction with the Damietta branch of the river. Here they were barely twenty miles from Cairo—every man with a spyglass turned it upon the distant outline of the pyramids—and Bonaparte, hearing at last from spies that the Mameluke army was waiting for him on the west bank outside Cairo, ordered a day's rest. On July 20 a twelve-hour forced march was begun before dawn, and the army bivouacked that night within a mile or two of Embaba. At 1 a.m. on July 21 the camp was already astir, and in the dawn light the soldiers saw the Mamelukes for the first time since Jibbrish: a thousand of them drawn up silently in line across the desert. Bonaparte went forward on horseback and surveyed the position through his glass. He saw beyond the enemy outposts the great camp at Embaba, and judged that there were about 20,000 enemy infantry there, with perhaps some forty guns in crude entrenchments. The chief interest in these guns for Bonaparte was that they were river-boat guns without wheels or carriages, and therefore immobile. To the west of the camp the bulk of the Mameluke cavalry appeared to be drawn up astride the road to the pyramids at Gizeh, and he judged them to number between 9,000 and 10,000. It was now 10 a.m. and the sun was rising to its full power.

There are many strange aspects about the Battle of the Pyramids; it took place, for example, nowhere near the pyramids—they were eight or nine miles away—and by the same process of romantic association most people remember this day because of Bonaparte's famous exhortation to his troops,[1] those

[1] "*Soldats! Du haut de ces monuments, quarante siècles vous regardent.*"—"Soldiers! From these monuments, forty centuries are watching you."

THE TISISAT FALLS

Photo: by courtesy of the Imperial Ethiopian Embassy

Photo: Scott, Edinburgh

JAMES BRUCE

MURAD BEY

BONAPARTE IN EGYPT

OZORO ESTHER

AN ETHIOPIAN CHIEFTAIN OF BRUCE'S TIME

ALEXANDRIA PORT IN 1798

THE ESBEKIAH SQUARE WHEN FLOODED

DESAIX

KLÉBER

THE BATTLE OF THE NILE AT THE START OF THE ACTION: THE FRENCH SHIPS IN THE CENTRE

DENON

Above: DENON (LEFT) SKETCHING IN THE DESERT
Below: FRENCH SCIENTISTS MEASURING THE SPHINX

MAMELUKES

THE EMPEROR THEODORE

Photo: Radio Times Hulton Picture Library

RASSAM

NAPIER

MEREWETHER

KASSAI

LOADING THE ELEPHANTS

THE RELEASED PRISONERS

same troops who were probably much too busy to pay any attention to it. Yet perhaps the really significant factor in the whole affair is that Bonaparte, in these outlandish circumstances, and still a young man of twenty-nine, should have divined in one instant, and apparently with absolute conviction, precisely what he had to do. Never was a battle more clearly planned. He sees the fixed guns in the enemy camp and decides at once to keep them out of the battle for the time being by remaining outside their range while he tackles the Mameluke cavalry in the open desert. If the enemy infantry choose to come to the aid of the cavalry by sallying out of their camp, then so much the better, they will have to fight without the aid of their artillery. If, however, the infantry decide to remain where they are, it seems not unlikely that he will defeat the Mameluke cavalry with his own mobile guns and the concentrated fire of his squares; and then it will be time enough to turn on the enemy camp. A French detachment placed behind the camp and astride the Gizeh road will prevent the remnants of the Mameluke cavalry from coming to the assistance of their infantry; and indeed the infantry themselves will have no place to which to retreat except into the Nile.

There seems to be no reason to doubt Bonaparte's word that this, in fact, was the way he designed the battle, since these dispositions were those which he actually carried out; at all stages of the action the Mamelukes reacted, not to their own plan (which was presumably to draw the French on to assault the camp while they charged in upon them from the flanks) but to Bonaparte's plan.

So now Desaix was sent off to meet the Mamelukes on the right flank, and it was a long business, a matter of three hours, before all was ready, his infantry marching in squares, with the artillery in between, the baggage to the center, his scouts at the front. Murad appears to have been confused at first about what was happening; at all events it was not until 2 p.m., when the sun was at its fiercest and a strong wind blowing from the north, that he realized that his cavalry was about to be cut off from his infantry. Then at last he gave the order to charge.

At least six thousand horsemen were involved in this movement, and it is probably true to say that it was the last great cavalry charge of the Middle Ages. The contemporary attempts to describe it both in words and in drawings are not very satisfactory; they leave one with a confused picture of the Muslim pennants flying over the horses' heads, of the Mamelukes in their enormous turbans and fluttering robes, each man leaning forward with a saber in his right hand, of the foot-attendants running beside them and of scores of camels laden with panniers of ammunition and weapons following on behind. But all this vanishes in a moment in clouds of dust and smoke, and the noise of the charge—the thousands of hoofs beating on the sand, the shouts, the drums and the bugles—becomes lost in the general uproar of cannon. Few eyewitnesses ever really see a battle or comprehend what is happening while it is being fought, every soldier is isolated in the small frantic world of his own experience, and this battle was more tumultuous than most, quicker in action, more savage in character and more concentrated in time; it was, indeed, one long crisis, while it lasted.

Desaix had just reached a sparse grove of palm trees when the charge began, and he had barely time to settle his soldiers into their action stations before the Mamelukes were upon them. They waited until the leading horsemen were within fifty paces. Then they fired. Denon speaks of the enemy riding right up to the mouths of the cannon before they fell or turned aside. Those who wheeled round the squares, seeking to make a breach in the sides and rear, were soon caught in the crossfire of Reynier's division that was coming up behind Desaix; and when they turned to charge again their frightened animals were buffeted back and forth from one square to another. Murad, who had put himself in the van of the first assault, escaped with a slight wound in his cheek, and he appears to have realized that the battle was lost almost before it had begun. He gathered together the remnants of his men and retired towards the pyramids. Desaix's cavalry following up behind soon got themselves behind the enemy camp at Embaba and took up a position close to the river bank.

Meanwhile Dugua's division, with Bonaparte in one of the squares, was advancing on the camp itself. They turned aside a cavalry charge, and seeing the way clear before them rushed straight upon the enemy guns which, up to this point, had taken no part in the battle. Nor were the gunners able to contribute much even at this desperate moment. They fired once, but before they could reload and fire again the French were on top of them, and a hand-to-hand struggle began among the entrenchments and the baggage of the camp. Murad attempted to come to the assistance of his infantry from the rear, but he found himself blocked by Desaix's division; and now in fact the bulk of the Mameluke army and its thousands of camp followers were surrounded. "From this moment," Denon says, "it was no longer a battle: it was a massacre."

Ibrahim, waiting with his reserves and a huge crowd of townspeople on the east bank, was appalled to see Embaba go up in flames, and presently out of the pall of the sandstorm raised by the north wind thousands of figures, Mamelukes as well as infantry, came running to the river. There were no boats, but apparently these men preferred death by drowning to the bullets of the French, and so they flung themselves into the choppy water, even rode their horses into it, and were soon swept away by the current. This was a great reassurance to the sailors in the French flotilla further down the river. All day they had been struggling against the current, hoping to take part in the action, but at the time of the Mamelukes' first charge they were still miles away. They heard in the distance a tremendous cannonade, and presently this grew fainter—a sign that the enemy were in retreat. But the wind dropped and the noise of the battle grew stronger than before and seemed much closer, almost as if it were Bonaparte who was falling back. In some alarm the sailors listened as the firing continued to increase, but now the bodies of the dead enemy began to float down towards them, at first in twos and threes and then in dozens—the Mamelukes in their gorgeous robes like great tropical flowers on the surface of the water—and they knew that the battle was won. It had been decided in a little more than an hour.

Back on the battlefield and around the camp at Embaba the French soldiers found that they had reached their eldorado at last. The Mamelukes had gone into action carrying their wealth with them. Some had as many as 300 or 400 gold louis in their saddlebags, and their equipment—the inlaid swords and daggers, the silk scarves and the jeweled turbans—were worth a fortune to men who earned only a few sous a day. There was no shortage of this loot; three, perhaps four, thousand Mamelukes and their men had been either killed or drowned, and few of the French failed to get a share; barely two hundred of their own number had fallen. In the camp itself all forty pieces of cannon were recovered intact, together with some 800 camels and baggage animals, large stores of food and many cases of silver and other treasure. It was a measure of the ferocity of the fighting and of the bravery of the Mamelukes that only 1,000 prisoners were taken.

It was still daylight. Murad, with about two thousand surviving cavalry, paused only a quarter of an hour at his country house near the pyramids and then continued on into the desert towards Beni Suef. Before he left, however, he found time to make one last gesture. There were about sixty boats anchored in the Nile above Rhoda Island, and before the battle they had been loaded with the Mamelukes' personal treasure. Seeing he had no time to man them and sail them away Murad now set fire to these vessels. Bonaparte, coming up to the river in the last light of the evening, saw a marvelous sight: the great grey pyramid of Cheops illumined by the flames, and in the distance, floating in the reflected glow, the domes and minarets of Cairo.

He moved into Murad's house with his staff, and there, in this moment of triumphant relaxation, roamed from room to room marveling at the cushions and the divans, the damask and the silk hangings fringed with gold. In the garden his officers fell upon the ripe bunches of grapes hanging from the vines.

Towards nine o'clock another, stronger glow lit up the sky, this time over Cairo itself. Ibrahim had not even waited until the French turned their guns upon him across the river; he had retreated directly into the city with his bodyguard, and these, having gathered up their women and portable belongings, had continued directly out of the city towards the east. All night long people streamed through the gates, the men with baggage on their heads, the women with children on their shoulders. A horse fetched a fortune. Only those who could not flee remained behind, for it was believed that the French on entering the city would carry out a general massacre. The refugees, however, fared hardly better than the Mamelukes who had retreated into the Nile: a few miles outside Cairo they were set upon by Bedouin and stripped of their belongings. Only Ibrahim with his column of armed Mamelukes was able to get safely through.

Cairo was now taken over by a mob. They burst into the beys' houses, one after another, Murad's as well as Ibrahim's, looting them of every movable object and in some cases setting fire to the empty shell of the building as well. It was the light of these fires which the French saw from across the river.

An Egyptian has described this as "the most horrible night of Cairo's history." For the French, however, it was the marvelous, almost unbelievable reward for the hardships of the past three weeks, and Bonaparte, his every promise to his men fulfilled, could sit down with some elation in Murad's house and write his dispatch to the Directory. It was the discipline of his men, he thought, that sangfroid which had enabled them to wait before firing until the Mamelukes had approached to within fifty paces of their ranks, that had won the day. One can imagine him lying down to sleep at last on one of Murad's divans, still dressed in his uniform. He had been awake for some twenty hours. It was a wonderful thing to be young.

CHAPTER SEVEN

THE OCCUPATION

BONAPARTE, after his Italian campaigns, was already an old hand in the business of dealing with captured cities, and the arrangements he now made at Cairo will be familiar to most soldiers who fought in the last world war. The frightened leaders of the community are sent for and are reassured that there will be no reprisals if no further resistance is offered; the shops must be reopened, law and order re-established, and billets made available to the soldiers who are to occupy the city. An officer is appointed as military governor, proclamations are pasted up on the walls, and presently the victorious soldiers come marching in. From the windows of their houses the people watch them silently and intently, fearing the worst, trying desperately to understand what the future is going to bring.

There is a certain arrogance in all soldiers occupying a conquered town. It is muted and disguised for the time being, nevertheless it is there; they despise the helpless, dejected civilians with their meek, averted faces and their shabby houses. This will change presently as the civilians grow more confident and the soldiers begin to feel the need of more human relationships, especially with the women. Food will be bought and paid for, strange faces and manners will grow familiar, and the civilians will learn how to placate their new rulers, how to use them for their own advantage, and perhaps eventually how to cheat them. For the moment, however, all is wariness and suspicious curiosity, with confidence on one side and fear on the other, and when at last the commander in chief comes riding into the city he appears to them all, soldiers and civilians alike, to be a very great man indeed, the symbol of absolute power, the final arbiter of all their lives.

These effects, which were now about to be produced in Cairo, were of extraordinary interest, not only because it was the French, the most talented people in Europe, who were the victors, and the Egyptians, by nature a devious and long-suffering race, who were the conquered, not only because of the astonishing rapidity of the collapse of the country, but because this was the first real meeting of the West and the East in Egypt since the departure of the Roman garrisons well over a thousand years before.

The negotiations were opened at dawn on Sunday, July 22. Having posted a division on Rhoda Island, which was divided only by a narrow channel from Cairo, Bonaparte sent a message to the sheikhs and imams to come to him at Gizeh. The ulema—the religious leaders—had not all fled the city, and they chose two of their number as their representatives. From these men Bonaparte learned that Ibrahim had gone, taking with him Abu Bekir Pasha, the Sultan's Viceroy. So it remained now to find others to take their place. The envoys were sent back to Cairo with assurances of peace, and were instructed that they must return with the leading men who had been left behind in the city. Next day, July 23, a deputation of sheikhs arrived, and after a conference of several hours offered their submission. General Dupuy was now appointed governor, and he followed the sheikhs back to the city. His soldiers occupied the port at Bulaq, the central part of Cairo, and the citadel, while he himself set up his headquarters in Ibrahim's house overlooking the Nile.

Now finally, when all was ready, Bonaparte himself entered Cairo to the sound of drums and trumpets, and the population came out to gaze on him as he rode by. A sumptuous place, the recently built house of Elfy Bey, one of the wealthiest of the departed Mamelukes, had been reserved for him in the center of the town, in Esbekiah Square. Here the commander in chief (or the Grand Sultan, the *Sultan Kebir*, as the Egyptians called him) lived in great style. His coachman Caesar caused much astonishment when he appeared in the narrow streets of Cairo with his coach and six.

Awakening from the daze created by the battle, the French and Egyptians now began to observe one another, and the Egyptians at first were immensely relieved. If the French had their mad idiosyncrasies, such as the order obliging the citizens to wear the cockade in their turbans, they were also generous, even to the point of naïveté: they paid for what they bought at very high prices, and the Egyptian bakers, full of wonder at such gullibility, soon began to mix earth with the flour and make smaller loaves. The bazaars and coffee-houses reopened, and many of those who had fled to the desert began to return.

There were excesses of course—despite Bonaparte's orders the French soldiers joined in the looting that was still going on—but the mosques were respected, and householders found that they could get an official paper from General Dupuy's office which, when pasted on the front door, was usually sufficient protection from the mob. During the next few days those Mamelukes who had gone into hiding were informed upon, arrested, and in some cases hanged, but their wives were protected and the French merely demanded of them a ransom—a pretty stiff ransom in the case of Fatima, Murad's wife: she had to pay 720,000 francs.

Bonaparte during these early days tried hard to make himself acceptable to his new subjects. A council of Egyptian elders was set up to replace the Mameluke beys, and a genuine effort was made to encourage them to govern. It was before this council that Bonaparte appeared in Egyptian costume—one marvels at the picture of that pale face beneath the enormous turban—and delivered a harangue on the equality and fraternity of mankind. At banquets he sat cross-legged among the sheikhs and ate with his fingers.

Egyptians were appointed as governors of the provinces, each with a French commissioner to assist him, and Bonaparte himself designed for these officials a splendid new uniform with a blue-plumed hat. Taxes were imposed on what was believed to be a fair and reasonable basis, and in the law courts and government offices an attempt was made to do away with the Mameluke system of corruption and bribery. Next, an elaborate scheme of public works was set on foot; canals were cleared, rubbish was removed from the streets, a bridge of boats was thrown across the Nile, and engineers repaired the hydraulic machine in the great octagonal tower that supplied the citadel with water. Troops were sent off to rescue a caravan of Mecca pilgrims who were being harassed by the Bedouin outside Cairo. In other words, this was the policy of appeasement, and what was to be attempted by the French was nothing less than the remaking of Egypt.

This was where the intellectuals were to play their part. At the opening meeting of the new Institute of Egypt Bonaparte accepted the vice-presidency, and he himself elected to direct the work of the department of mathematics. The Institute's program would have done credit to UNESCO and all the combined agencies of United Nations as well. In the field of arts they were to study the monuments and the antiquities, to write a history of ancient Egypt, to prepare a French-Egyptian dictionary and to publish two journals. In engineering they were to devise one plan for the cutting of the Suez Canal and another for the preservation of fresh water by the erection of a series of dams on the Nile. The causes of the annual flooding of the river were also to be examined. In agriculture they were to experiment with new crops, in medicine they were to investigate the disease of the eyes and to reorganize the sanitary and hospital services; in economy a new scheme of weights and measures was to be devised. Others were to busy themselves with such matters as the desert mirage, the hippopotamus and the crocodile, and the movements of heavenly bodies in the bright Egyptian sky. A census was to be carried out, the country accurately mapped, and a study made of geology and natural history. Egypt, for the first time, was to be revealed to itself and to the world.

It seems clear that the Egyptians themselves, on recovering from the first shock of the conquest, neither liked nor approved of any of these dealings. Bonaparte and his intellectuals were moved by the ardent revolutionary principle that all men wished to be free and to improve themselves, but this, as we have seen, was not necessarily the case in a country that had scarcely ever known either freedom or improvement. The Egyptian sheikhs and imams had no wish to take on the responsibility of government, they were frightened of it. They had had their own devious system for survival under the Mamelukes, and what the French appeared to be offering them was not freedom but a new sort of subservience, worse than the one they had known before because it was alien and strange. The Mamelukes had been lax in gathering taxes, but the French were proving very thorough; they employed Copts and Greeks to ferret out the last piastre, and it was difficult to come to some comfortable arrangement with a bribe. Everything these new conquerors proposed was a strain; it was a strain *not* to throw rubbish in the streets, *not* to bribe witnesses and officials, and it was upsetting to be obliged to undergo medical treatment where prayers had always served in the past. They had been getting on very well, they felt, as they were before. They had no need for new canals, new weights and measures, and new schools. Above all, they hated Christian interference in their private lives. They did not believe Bonaparte's protestations of his respect for Muhammad, nor were they much impressed by his dressings-up in turban and caftan or the great celebrations he ordered for the birthday of the Prophet; every move his soldiers made was an affront to the Muhammadan way of life.

A contemporary Egyptian observer said, "Cairo has become a second Paris; women go about shamelessly with the French; intoxicating drinks are publicly sold and things are committed of which the Lord of heaven would not approve."

The French on their side were no better pleased with the situation than the Egyptians, once the first glow of victory was over. Campaigning with Bonaparte in Italy they had moved among familiar scenes where the inhabitants behaved more or less as they did themselves. But here they were surrounded by dark shuttered houses, by women who in general revealed nothing of themselves but their eyes and the tips of their fingers, by people whose language and religion were a mystery, whose celebrations were gibberish and whose food was uneatable. They had had no mail from home since they had sailed three months before, and now that the first pressure of the campaign was over many of the men fell ill. They were forever hot and uncomfortable, and it was not long before they were beset by that bane of all occupying armies: restlessness and boredom. Bonaparte drew up a list of requirements he wanted urgently from France: a company of comedians, a troupe of ballet dancers, a marionette show, two hundred thousand pints of brandy and a million of wine. Meanwhile a kind of pleasure-garden was set up in one of the squares of the city.

No one could stir without an escort. Not even the Nile was safe; the Bedouin waited on the banks until the wind dropped or the boats ran on a sandbank. Then they pounced. In these circumstances even Bonaparte's dispatches were failing to get through, and he had received no word from the Directory since he had sailed. And so each day the malcontents grew in number, and they could talk of nothing except how they could return to France.

But no one could return to France, not for a long time yet. It was soon realized that the campaign which had opened so brilliantly had only just begun, and was about to enter a new phase; in place of pitched battles which were short and victorious they were faced with guerrilla warfare which promised to be long and hard. Bonaparte sent a message to Murad, who had reached the Fayoum oasis, offering him the governorship of Upper Egypt if he would submit, but Murad merely replied with a counter-offer; he said he would pay the French a ransom if they would get out of Egypt. Nor did Bonaparte have any better luck with the Mamelukes who had gone east: when he proposed to Abu Bekir Pasha that he should return to Cairo and resume his role as the Sultan's Viceroy he received no reply at all. The Pasha by now was well on his way to Syria with Ibrahim, each of them with enormous baggage in his train, and they had no intention of returning.

Ibrahim at least, Bonaparte decided to destroy. He himself

joined the detachment that set off in pursuit, and although they caught up with Ibrahim's escort, Ibrahim himself and Abu Bekir escaped and continued on their way. Bonaparte spent two days organizing his provincial administration, and it was on his journey back to Cairo that at last he received word from the garrison he had left behind at Alexandria under Kléber. It is said that he read Kléber's message with an air of imperturbability, and if this is true it is remarkable, for it contained terrible news, the worst that could possibly be: the French fleet at Alexandria had been utterly destroyed by the English. The expedition was cut off from France.

"On the morning of July 31, 1798," Denon, one of the intellectuals, wrote, "the French were masters of Egypt, Corfu and Malta; thirty vessels of the line united these possessions with France." Now on August 1, the day on which the battle of the Nile was fought (though Bonaparte did not hear of it until eleven days later), "the Army of the East was imprisoned in its own conquest." Overnight the French had become marooned colonists instead of conquerors.

It was many days before the details of the battle reached Cairo. Admiral Brueys had been unwilling to take his ships into Alexandria harbor until its narrow entrance had been charted, and Bonaparte declares that before he began his march to Cairo on July 6 he left definite instructions for the admiral: if he could not get into port he was to discharge his cargoes as best he might and then sail for Corfu. At Corfu he would be safe from the British. Bonaparte in his memoirs goes on to say that he repeated these instructions later, but that instead of obeying them Brueys, still unable or unwilling to go into Alexandria, remained loitering for three weeks in the open sea of Abukir Bay, about fifteen miles to the northeast of the city; and there Nelson caught him.

All this remains true enough, but it is hardly fair to Brueys. Bonaparte's repeated instructions did not get through to him in time; during the whole period that the French army was making its way up to Cairo Brueys had no news at all from Bonaparte. He did not know what had happened to the French army. It was conceivable that it had been defeated and would have to be re-embarked. In those circumstances he could not abandon it and sail for Corfu. And so his ships, anchored by the bow and two hundred and fifty yards apart, remained in a curve about one and three-quarters of a mile long off the coast between Abukir Island and the Rosetta mouth of the Nile. The vessels were at all times ready for action, but their decks were still cluttered with cabins rigged up for the soldiers, a third or more of the crews were on shore, many were ill (Brueys himself was unwell) and morale was low.

Nelson, after leaving Alexandria at the end of June, had doubled back to Sicily in search of the French, and it was only on his arrival at Syracuse on July 19 that he heard that they were in Egypt. Having watered and provisioned his squadron of fourteen vessels, he sailed again for Alexandria and arrived in sight of the French fleet towards dusk on August 1. The sun and the breeze were behind him, the sea was calm. He conceived the dangerous plan of splitting his force into two squadrons, one squadron to run between the French and the shore, the other to go into action from the open sea, and he attacked at once.

The term "The Battle of the Nile" is another romantic misnomer, since it was not fought on the Nile at all or even at the mouth of the river: it was fought in the Abukir roadstead, where the French had been stationed for weeks. But no one has ever questioned the rightness of Nelson's plan or the brilliance of his victory. As each of his 74s came into range they anchored, and a tremendous broadside swept the French, undermanned as they were, from two directions at once. At 8 p.m. Brueys was wounded on the quarterdeck of his flagship *Tonnant*, and at 9 p.m. he died. The British *Bellerophon* engaged *L'Orient*, the ship of the line in which Bonaparte had sailed from France, and was disabled, but at 10 p.m. *L'Orient* herself blew up with a loud explosion. Thereafter there was a long silence under the full moon and the bright stars, but those watching on shore could see nothing because of the thick clouds of smoke drifting over the water, and presently the cannonading began again.

The dawn revealed a scene of frightful wreckage. Nine British ships were dismasted and 218 of their crews were dead, with 678 more wounded. Nelson himself was hit on the head by a ball. But the French were annihilated. Of Brueys' thirteen ships of the line and fourteen frigates only four—two 74s and two frigates—were not sunk, captured, or lying unmanageable on the water, and these four, cutting their cables, managed to escape. For days afterwards bodies and wreckage of every kind kept drifting on to the shore, there to be seized upon by the Bedouin. No one ever accurately computed the French losses. It is known, however, that about 3,500 of the surviving sailors joined Bonaparte's army in Egypt.

Nelson remained for two and a half weeks off Abukir, landing the prisoners taken in the battle, and refitting six prizes for their voyage to England, and then, leaving Hood to establish a blockade, himself sailed for Naples. He had dealt Bonaparte a blow from which any other commander would never have recovered.

In one unexpected way the very magnitude of the disaster was of assistance to the French. It left them without an alternative: being now cut off from all hope of returning to France, they concentrated their energies upon Egypt and began to accept a life of exile. This of course did not prevent the soldiers and the camp followers from sending the most dismal letters home. Egypt, they assured their families, was the vilest and most inhospitable of countries, its people scurrilous and dirty, its landscape nothing but arid desert, its towns filled with horrible disease. Even Bonaparte gave way at times to fits of despair. Writing a little later on to his brother Joseph he spoke of his prospects of escaping:

"In two months it is possible that I shall be back in France, so find me a house where I may spend the winter alone. I am sick of humanity: I need solitude and isolation. Greatness wearies me, emotion chills me, my passion for glory has vanished. At twenty-nine years of age I am worn out."

Such letters as these were dispatched by frigates from Alexandria, and often these frigates were intercepted by the

British blockade, which soon after the Battle of the Nile had been reinforced by Turkish and Russian ships. Already the British were predisposed to think that it was only a matter of time before the French expedition collapsed of its own misfortunes, and these letters seemed to confirm that view. There was no need, it was thought, to land a British force in Egypt; the Turks, who had now declared war on Bonaparte, would be able to deliver the *coup de grâce* without assistance. Nelson gave it as his opinion that the French could be forced to surrender within three months.

Now in point of fact the French army was very far from being desperate. It suffered hardly at all from the lack of supplies from France; the soldiers were being amply and well fed from the rich fields of the delta, perhaps better fed than they would have been at home, and gradually, with the welcome prospect of the mild Egyptian winter before them, they were acclimatizing themselves. They had captured a quantity of guns and arms of every kind, in addition to transport animals and river-boats; a factory for the manufacture of gunpowder had been set up, and such articles as boots and uniforms could easily be made in Egypt. The army's losses had been very few; despite sickness the original force of some 36,000 men was still almost intact. To these Bonaparte added local levies of Greeks and Copts, who could be used for garrison duties and in the transport corps.

Now too Bonaparte began to perceive that his appeasement policy could never convert the Egyptians into active allies or partners. They could be ruled and coerced but never persuaded, or absolutely trusted. He began to take a harsher line with the sheikhs. The citizens of Cairo now found they had to have a license for every activity in life, for buying and selling, for the registration of a birth, a marriage or a death, for the transfer of property—and these licenses had to be paid for. The discussion of politics was forbidden, and communication with the Mamelukes was made punishable by death. All mules had to be sold as transport animals to the army, and a private citizen found with an animal was fined 1,800 francs. The dead could no longer be buried outside the houses, they had to be taken to the tombs of the Mamelukes outside the city; and amid the fearful screams of the women French soldiers began to tear up the graves in the Esbekiah Square. A quarantine station detained travelers at Bulaq, and as a further precaution against the plague letters had to be dipped in vinegar and every house and its contents were ordered to be cleaned within fifteen days.

One after another the new edicts were shouted through the streets by town criers, and the French soldiers, who imagined that they had come as liberators, now feared to walk about without arms.

The question of the lamps caused as much exasperation as anything; it was the reverse of the black-out regulations in the last world war. Every house was ordered to hang out a lamp at night, and if the light went out a police patrol would at once nail up the door. It remained closed until a fine was paid. Egyptian lamps were primitive affairs, prone to continual failure, and soon the whole town was in a state of resentful agitation—it was even said that the police extinguished the lights themselves in order to raise money.

Bonaparte called a halt in some cases (he settled the lamp affair by putting official lights in the streets and he stopped the desecration of the Esbekiah graves), but now, at last, the Egyptians were beginning to know the true nature of western occupation, which was government enforced by military law. A cannon shot woke the city every morning at daybreak.

The commander in chief continued to be very confident. Far from thinking of surrender he set about redesigning Cairo, building new boulevards, no doubt with Paris in mind; he established a mint, and he visited Suez on horseback in order to put his great project for the canal on foot.[1]

Conté, the balloonist, managed to get a tricolored balloon into the air, and his windmills, the first to be seen in Egypt, were another demonstration of the marvelous inventiveness of the French.

But it was the Nile that preoccupied Bonaparte's mind. He

[1] It was abandoned when Lepère, his engineer, reported (erroneously) that the scheme was impossible because the Red Sea was some thirty feet higher than the Mediterranean.

might be able to exist for the time being without contact with France, but it was impossible for him to remain secure in the delta so long as the Mamelukes had control of the river to the south. At any moment they could mount a counterattack from Upper Egypt; and in fact it was known that Murad was already assembling a new army there. He might not have stood a chance in a pitched battle against the French, but guerrilla warfare was another matter. He had taken some 2,000 Mamelukes with him to the Fayoum oasis together with about 5,000 irregular Arab cavalry, and he could count to some extent on the assistance of the Bedouin and of the tribes living along the river bank. This was an ample force for armed raids into the delta, perhaps even for the siege of Cairo itself. He was in contact by courier with the malcontents in Cairo and Alexandria and with Ibrahim in Syria, and every week the ancient cry for a jihad, a holy war to expel the infidel, was growing stronger. By the middle of August it was apparent that the French would have no peace in the delta until Murad was either destroyed or driven so far off that sheer distance made him harmless. So now, in the midst of his activities in Cairo, Bonaparte began to prepare for a campaign on the river.

It has been the fate of this new adventure to be regarded as a sideshow in the French expedition to Egypt, and so it was, militarily speaking; not more than five thousand French were involved, and Murad at no time commanded more than about ten to fourteen thousand men. And yet this campaign was to accomplish wonderful things. It was to unlock the forgotten culture and history of the ancient Egyptian past for the first time since the days of the Romans; it was to prepare the way for the penetration of the modern world further and further upstream until the whole mystery of the river system was at last explained, the White Nile as well as the Blue.

Perhaps one of the reasons why the campaign has been so overlooked is that Bonaparte himself did not accompany it; nearly all his senior generals and the historians who were later to write about their deeds remained with the commander in chief in Cairo. The Nile expedition was a campaign within a campaign, and nobody in Europe knew or cared anything about it; England and her allies were concentrated upon Bonaparte and the Mediterranean. And so for fourteen months the two little armies, alien to one another in every aspect of their being, were locked away from the rest of the world on the upper reaches of the river between the pyramids and Philae.

Desaix, who was now recognized as second only to Bonaparte himself as a field commander, was given the French command, and his orders were quite simple: he was to pursue Murad and destroy him on the Upper Nile. To start with he was to have 3,000 infantry, about 100 guns, 1,000 cavalry, and a little fleet of boats and a camel train to convey him up the river. General Belliard, who had accompanied Desaix from Civitavecchia, was to be the second-in-command.

Spies were sent on ahead into the Fayoum oasis, but in general everything on the Nile was unknown to the French. The general circumstances of the adventure that lay ahead—the shoals and currents in the river, the rise and fall of the water, the language and the nature of the inhabitants, the heat by day and the cold by night, the sandstorms and the mirages that could always turn out to be the enemy on the horizon, the possibility of finding food and fodder, the existence of forts and of ancient cities that could bar their progress, and the ultimate course of the great river that led them on, seemingly forever, to the south—all this was a mystery that could only be revealed little by little through their own experience, and always in the presence of an enemy who was ready at any moment to strike and then vanish into the desert.

Now, however, the river was high and the wind still conveniently from the north. The boats were loaded, the camel train mustered on the bank, and on August 25 Desaix set out.

One of the last men to join the expedition was Denon, a queer fish in this operation, since he was a civilian and already aged fifty-one, and therefore something of an oddity among these aggressive young soldiers of the revolutionary army. He was not really interested in war at all, nor even in the present: he was absorbed in the past. Dominique Vivant Denon-Baronde, to give him his full name, had been everything in his time, playwright, artist, diplomat, archaeologist, interior decorator (he had designed some of the revolutionary uniforms), and now a friend of Bonaparte. Having belatedly followed the army up to Cairo from Alexandria, he went straight on to the pyramids, since an escort of 200 soldiers had been dispatched there at that moment, and it was unsafe to make the excursion alone. Now, after a month of investigations in Cairo, terrier-like in its intensity, he hurried on, as the representative of the Institute of Egypt, in the wake of Desaix's men. Through the next ten months he was to prove to be the best of observers, and one of the ablest of pioneers in discovering the ancient past of the river.

CHAPTER EIGHT

THE CAMPAIGN ON THE RIVER

FOR Desaix's little army the Nile valley was a hard and hostile place, and as the soldiers advanced along it they experienced all the brutal realities of life as it was actually lived on the river, whether by invading armies in the past or by the present Egyptians. They ate the native food, drank the Nile water, and camped in the Egyptian houses. Every village had to be reconnoitered, captured or placated, every tomb was the possible hiding place of an enemy. The climate had not altered—the blinding heat of August in Upper Egypt, the sandstorms and the glare—and the march seemed endless; the desert rocks were so hard that each soldier required a new pair of boots every month. At the very outset of the campaign Desaix exclaims: "Never have I seen the men so tired."

It was no wonder. They were still dressed in heavy serge, with a collar round the neck—and how spectacular those crimson and yellow facings must have looked in this bright sunlight—and all of them at one time or another appear to have suffered from dysentery and eye disease. Each morning reveille sounded between 2 and 3 a.m., and they were forever on the move, forever fighting, looking for billets, fetching water, cooking, getting up again.

The scenes they saw along the Nile were not quite the same as those we see now. The villages, though smaller, have not altered much in the intervening years, but the ancient temples were then very different. Many were half-buried in sand, and successive generations of Arabs had built mud-brick houses among the crumbling walls, throwing out their rubbish everywhere. No one cared for these old columns and statues, no one could read the hieroglyphics on the walls. The mummies hidden in their hundreds of underground caves were of interest solely because the resin with which they were impregnated could be extracted and sold in the Cairo market. The fallen obelisk was simply another rock.

In a way perhaps all this was an advantage. A certain staleness overtakes great monuments that have been too much excavated and restored and then photographed, painted and walked over by millions of tourist feet. But for a man like Denon in 1798 everything was fresh and wonderful. Reading his account of the campaign it is impossible not to feel something of his own excitement as he groped his way down dark passages with a lamp and saw, as few eyes had seen for a thousand years or more, great underground chambers filled with statues and paintings that were still brightly colored, and mystical inscriptions all around them on the walls. One understands how he marveled at the sight of huge forgotten temples rising out of the sand.

Denon was lucky to find in both Desaix and Belliard men with educated and inquiring minds, who were ready and even eager to indulge him, but the war had to be fought, and it was hardly ever safe for him to linger. No sooner would he begin a sketch or start to trace an inscription than the trumpet would sound the advance, and he would have to scramble onto his horse and hurry after the others. To have remained alone behind the army meant more or less certain death from the Bedouin, and on several occasions Denon had to gallop off through a fusillade of shots.

The army's problems were more exacting. The Mamelukes, after one more futile charge at Fayoum, came to their senses at last and realized that their best means of harassing and even of defeating the French lay in guerrilla tactics. They knew the country and the French did not. The French were impeded by heavy baggage and stores, while the Mamelukes, although accompanied by their wives and followers, traveled light, despoiling the land behind them as they fell back. There was every possible advantage to Murad in extending Desaix to the utmost by retreating further and further up the Nile. By doubling back on his tracks through the empty desert, he was then able to cut in on Desaix's line of communication; and this, in a haphazard way, was what Murad now set himself out to do. So what we have to contemplate here is a disjointed running battle on the river. It ranges up and down the Nile as far as Philae, nearly six hundred miles from Cairo, and spreads at times far into the surrounding desert; and it is marvelous that Desaix, far from despairing, never for an instant gave up the chase. "I think," said one of his officers, "that General Desaix is ten degrees colder than ice," and one remembers Desaix's own admiring comment on Bonaparte: "He follows his enemy to the end of the world."

The beginning of the campaign did not altogether go against the Mamelukes. After leaving Cairo Desaix's boats had much trouble with shoals and sandbanks in the falling Nile, and it was not until October 6 that he caught up with Murad at a place called El-Lahun. Through his glass he could see Murad himself, sitting outside his tent with his sheikhs on one of the neighboring heights. They soon retired, however, and Desaix, having spent all the following day getting his boats up, ordered the men to sleep at arms that night and in their squares. On the morning of October 8 he moved forward in battle formation towards Murad's entrenchments, and the leading men had barely got themselves onto a slight rise when a drum was heard in the enemy camp, and dust, rising from under their horses' hoofs, made it evident that the Mamelukes were coming in for a charge.

The odds against Murad were not so weighted as they had been in the Battle of the Pyramids. Then he had faced some 20,000 Frenchmen. Now he saw barely 3,000 before him, and his own forces at this time outnumbered them nearly two to one. Desaix had placed his men in a curious arrangement: two small squares of 180 men each were deployed in front, while the rest, with their artillery, remained in one solid mass behind. The commander of the foremost small square ordered his men to hold their fire until the Mamelukes were only twenty paces away, and this was foolish, because the wounded horsemen in the van were carried by their own impetus into the square, and other Mamelukes, following behind, rushed into the breach. Some twenty of the French infantry were quickly hacked down. The rest, however, had sufficient presence of mind to lie full length on the sand, and this enabled the French artillery to fire over them into the mass of enemy cavalry. A further Mameluke charge on the second small square was held, but by now Murad had one of his own batteries in action, and the French were obliged to rush it with the bayonet before it was silenced. After this the Mamelukes retreated, leaving about four hundred of their men, dead and wounded, on the field.

The chase was now on. Any soldier who campaigned in the desert in the last world war will remember the exhilaration of pursuing a retreating enemy there. The soldiers and the leading columns have an overmastering desire to go on and on, just another mile or two before sunset, just one more view over the next ridge of sand. It is like some mad treasure hunt, except that here the clues are the discarded baggage of the enemy, the broken guns beside the track, a deserted camp where the cooking fires are still warm, a furrow of recent wheel-tracks leading off into the distance.

Something of this sort now happened to the French. By the end of December they were in Assiut, one of the principal towns of the Nile, 250 miles upstream from Cairo. Soon after New Year's Day, 1799, they were on the move again, the men marching on the west bank and the flotilla following on the river, and on January 19 they were in Girga.

Murad had kept just ahead of them all the way. Sometimes he waited until the French were only an hour or two behind him before moving on; sometimes his outriders would turn back and cut in upon an isolated French detachment, but then after a quick skirmish they would be gone again. Like Desaix himself, and indeed like every army commander who has fought on the Nile, Murad was having trouble with his transport. But then he had allies among the local population. The Bedouin and many of the villagers were quite ready to oppose the invaders in the hope of pillage. Denon speaks of the French being "exhausted by daily losses and fatigued by victories," in a country where the enemy was "always conquered but never subjugated," and who "came on the morrow of a defeat to harass." Every night thieves "entered the French camp like rats and left it like bats." Even Desaix's horse was stolen.

Yet the French morale was high. For the most part they were moving through cultivated fields and gardens, food was plentiful—Assiut in fact was so rich that not even the presence of three thousand foreign soldiers forced up the price of chickens and fruit—and everything else the men lacked they looted from the villagers.

Now, in the winter, the heat by day was much more bearable and the nights were pleasantly cool. Once a rare thunderstorm burst upon them with heavy showers of rain, but this was refreshing. The French soldiers were now beginning to know their enemy very well. Hardly a man did not possess loot of some kind—a battle-axe, a quiver lined in red velvet, an amulet or a piece of brocade—and they had long since learned to distinguish the beys from the ordinary Mamelukes, since the beys wore beards.

At Girga Desaix had been strengthened by the arrival of additional cavalry with his supply boats, and he now resolved to push on after Murad at greater speed. A series of forced marches was ordered, mostly by night.

The final and terrible march was to Aswan, their last hope of catching Murad before he escaped into the deserts of Nubia beyond the Egyptian border. Craving for food and their feet dreadfully blistered, the soldiers crossed the river and entered Aswan on February 1, 1799, to find themselves too late: Murad had gone up the cataracts and had vanished into the unknown wastes that lay beyond. The army was now 587 miles from Cairo, and for the time being strained to the limit of its endurance. Desaix broke off the pursuit and settled into the town.

During the next few weeks Aswan must have borne some resemblance to what it was in Roman times. A fort was built, and a rather grandiose plaque was erected to commemorate the French victories on the river. They set up cafés and eating houses in Aswan and made the best of the local beer. Having no playing cards they designed their own, and they gambled with their loot. They explored the ruins and carved their names in the stone precisely as the Romans had done a thousand years before. While Desaix went off to organize a chain of posts down the river to Assiut, General Belliard set up a government, and once again the local people saw western soldiers parading with their bands in the early morning. Spies were sent up above the cataracts and reported that Murad was laying waste the river villages in Nubia, and presently there was news that he was approaching Aswan with a foraging party. At once a French column marched out to meet him, and they surprised the Mamelukes at their evening meal. But it was impossible to come to grips in the darkness, and in the morning the enemy were gone. It seemed for the time being that the war was over.

And now the heat was beginning again. "It boiled our blood . . . Nothing is as frightful as this death: the victim is suddenly surprised with a disorder of his heart and no assistance can save him from the faintings that succeed."

Moreover the French were much deluded in thinking that Murad had been defeated. At the end of February they had word that, with some hundreds of Mamelukes still in his train, he had made a wide detour through the desert and was descending again from Nubia into Egypt.

The next seven months are a confused story of marches and countermarches along the Nile valley between Aswan and Fayoum, of ambushes and violent skirmishes on the river. One can hardly fail to sympathize with Murad. He is not Robin Hood, and the Mamelukes were scarcely a merry lot, but they were men fighting for what they believed to be their rights, their pride and indignation were equal to every weariness, and they never gave up. This was the end of a tradition of five hundred years of Mameluke rule in Egypt, and it had its moments of nobility. Even the wounded would accept no mercy, and preferred to die fighting so long as there was a hope of killing just one more Frenchman.

Murad once managed to seize a flotilla of French ammunition boats, and even Bonaparte's diabeyah, *L'Italie*, was blown up. In one particularly drastic encounter seventy dragoons were killed, and Desaix, desperate for reinforcements, was moved to write bitterly to Bonaparte: "Eye troubles are frightening. I am deprived of more than 1,400 men, 100 of them blind.... We are naked, without shoes, without anything.... But I won't bore you with our sufferings."

By June 1799, however, Desaix could fairly claim that he had the upper hand. For nearly five hundred miles he was keeping the enemy off the river, and many of the local sheikhs had submitted. A headquarters was set up at Assiut to administer the vast territory that had been conquered, and trade was beginning to flow again along the Nile.

Denon went back to Cairo to report to the Institute on the scientific and cultural results of the campaign, and he had a wonderful story to tell. He had been defeated in the end in some of his inquiries; he had not been able to capture a baby crocodile, and many hours spent in putrid tunnels had failed to yield him a mummy intact. But he had brought back with him hundreds of drawings of temples, tombs and inscriptions, and an encyclopaedic volume of notes that ranged from a study of the sandstorms and the plagues of locusts to the nilometer at Aswan and the habits of the cave dwellers. He had also secured a number of ancient Egyptian manuscripts which later were to play their part, together with the Rosetta Stone (which had just been unearthed at the mouth of the river and brought to Cairo), in the deciphering of the ancient Egyptian hieroglyphics.

It was a moment of stalemate in the campaign. One must envisage a chain of little garrisons dotted up the Nile and divided from one another by about fifty miles or more, the tents pitched on the green bank, the barber and the drinking shops set up in the mud-hut villages, the cow-dung cooking fires under the palms with the French soldiers sitting round them in the evening, the occasional banquets offered to the officers by the local sheikhs—a strange mixture of tight uniforms and flowing robes, of French and Arabic—the daily rumors and alarms, the sick lying derelict through endless hot nights, the commotion of the arrival of a boat with supplies from Cairo but never with mail from home, the facetious signposts erected in the camp: "Route de Paris, No. 1"—the Paris that was impenetrably blocked from them by the desert and the sea beyond. This was exile in its deepest monotony, and no doubt it was only made bearable by the routine of drill and work, by an occasional whiff of danger and by the hope, never quite lost, that some miracle would happen to make it end.

They were establishing a legend of course, the glory of revolutionary France on the Nile, but one wonders whether this stirred the private soldier very much or even went far to compensate him for those famous promised six acres which, like France itself, were steadily receding into the distance. But human beings it seems will put up with anything, and from one dull day to the next these soldiers went on accepting their isolation and obeying their orders. They were gasping in the terrible summer heat of the Upper Nile. They hated it and they longed for it to end. And so there must have been a certain stir throughout the column when in July 1799 the calm was broken: Murad suddenly reappeared in Fayoum, evidently heading for the delta.

Desaix at once marched north in pursuit, and at the same time another French column came out from Cairo, hoping to intercept Murad before he could reach the delta; now at last they seemed to have him in a trap. July 13 was a dramatic day: Murad was reported to be in the vicinity of the pyramids, and Bonaparte himself hurried to the scene.

During the eleven months that Desaix had been away in Upper Egypt so much had happened to Bonaparte that one can only marvel that he should have kept his sanity. He had received no help from France of any kind. Russia, Turkey and England had combined against him, and the blockade continued on the coast. Yet he had managed to put down a serious rising in Cairo, he had made a disastrous expedition into Syria, where he had been stopped at Acre by the Turks and Sir Sidney Smith, and now, apparently unshaken, he was back in Cairo again, his army still more or less intact and Egypt still under control. There had been rumors of a Turkish invasion, but he appears to have been confident enough at this moment to turn all his attention to the capture of Murad.

Now in point of fact the rumor of the arrival of the Turks was entirely true. A fleet with sixty transports and an army of 20,000 men was actually about to arrive in Abukir Bay near Alexandria, and Murad had come north with the intention of joining forces with it there. It is not entirely clear how Murad had received word of the approach of the Turks, but it is certain that his wife Fatima had had a hand in the matter. Messengers were constantly passing to and fro between her house and Constantinople and her husband in Upper Egypt, and she herself may even have been at the center of a conspiracy to raise a new rebellion against the French, once the Turks were safely ashore at Abukir. On July 13, at all events, she was at her country estate at Gizeh, and Murad by arrangement is said to have climbed to the top of the Great Pyramid and to have signaled to her there.

Now was the moment for the French to pounce, and Bonaparte in fact was deploying his men when couriers arrived from Alexandria with the news of the Turkish landing. Murad had the pleasure of seeing the French army abruptly turn about and march directly for the coast. He himself followed discreetly in the rear.

The Battle of Abukir was not by a long way the most important victory of Bonaparte's career, but certainly he never fought with such devastating effect. On July 20 he was at Rahmaniya, and having paused there for a day or two to await the arrival of his reserves he advanced directly on Abukir with 10,000 men and 1,000 cavalry. The Turks had already killed the French garrison on the shore, and had established a beachhead, but they appear to have been poorly armed; they had no cavalry, no modern artillery, and no bayonets for their rifles. At dawn on July 25 Bonaparte attacked, and in the massacre that followed something like 15,000 Turks were killed, captured or drowned in a headlong flight into the sea. Mustapha Pasha, the

Turkish commander, was taken prisoner in his tent. Not even the Mamelukes had fared as badly as this, not even Nelson could claim a more decisive victory. When Murad heard the news he turned about and rode back into Upper Egypt, with Desaix still at his heels.

But the Mamelukes were now growing very tired. Early in August Desaix surprised their camp far up the river at Samhud, and Murad himself was so near being captured that he left behind him in his tent his arms, his clothes, even his slippers. A month later he was still on the run when Desaix's camel corps overtook him near Fayoum. But this was the end. A short sharp skirmish was fought, and soon afterwards a message was received from Fatima saying that her husband was prepared to negotiate. By the terms of his submission he agreed to serve under the French.

It was now mid-October 1799, and Desaix could look back on his achievements with some pride; those Mamelukes who had not surrendered with Murad were cut off and helpless in the deserts of Nubia, and from Philae to Cairo there was peace on the river at last. In a little more than a year, and with a force of barely five thousand men, he had conquered a territory half as large as France.

In this book our course is on the Nile, and so we need do no more here than glance at events in Egypt during the next ten years. Soon after the Battle of Abukir Bonaparte had news at last from France, and it was appalling: the French army in Italy was in retreat, the Ionian Islands had been taken by the Turks, Malta was blockaded and in Paris the political situation was chaotic. He decided to return to France at once, leaving Kléber in command in Egypt.

The arrangements for his flight were made with great secrecy; it was given out that he was to make a tour of inspection on the Lower Nile. Soon after midnight on August 18, 1799, three days after his thirtieth birthday, he went on board a boat at Bulaq to sail down the Nile to Alexandria.

At Alexandria the two frigates *Murion* and *Carrière* were waiting. It had been Bonaparte's intention to meet Kléber at

Rosetta and inform him that he was to take over the Egyptian command, but on August 21 he was warned that he must sail at once; the wind was favorable and the two British frigates that had been lurking off Alexandria had gone to Cyprus to revictual. There was time only to write to Kléber, "I will arrive in Paris, I will chase out this gang of lawyers who mock us and who are incapable of governing the Republic and I will consolidate this magnificent colony." Kléber was to hold on until reinforcements reached him. Only if they failed to arrive by May 1800, or if by then he had lost fifteen hundred men through plague, was he to negotiate with the Turks.

Early on August 22 Bonaparte boarded the *Murion*, which was waiting two miles out from the same beach at Marabu where he had first come ashore in Egypt fourteen months before. All his fellow passengers agree that the general was in the best of spirits on the hazardous voyage home. As they ran along the North African coast to Cape Bon he played *vingt-et-un*, discussed geometry and physics and drew them all into his schemes for the future. They hardly saw another ship until they touched in at Corsica, and then, on October 9, seven weeks after leaving Egypt, ran in through the British blockade to St. Raphael. A month later Bonaparte was dictator of France.

Kléber, abandoned in Egypt and bitterly resentful of Bonaparte's departure, not unreasonably saw very little point in waiting until fifteen hundred of his men had died of plague. Soon after the new year he opened negotiations with the Turks and the British at El Arish, and they reached an understanding that the French should leave Egypt, taking their arms with them and with the honors of war. It was the happiest possible end to the affair but it was a little too precipitous to satisfy the hatreds and passions that had been aroused; the British government wanted harsher terms and repudiated the agreement. This was a decision of the utmost folly, since it condemned Egypt to another eighteen months of war, and in the end, after another few thousand men were dead, the British found themselves obliged to agree to almost the same terms they had rejected at El Arish.

At last, in March 1801, a mixed force of British and Turks landed near Alexandria, and although the French garrison there managed to hold out for a time Cairo collapsed without a struggle.

It was thought surprising at the time that the French should have put up so little resistance—Belliard, who was now in command in Cairo, had 12,000 men and ample provisions—but by then their case was hopeless. The French army was sick of Egypt. All the best generals had gone: Kléber had been assassinated by a fanatic in Cairo on June 14, 1800, that same day on which Desaix, who had managed to rejoin Bonaparte in Europe, was killed at the battle of Marengo. Murad had remained faithful to his new alliance with the French, and was actually marching to Belliard's assistance from the Upper Nile, but he died of plague on the way. Soon too another British force landed from India on the Red Sea coast, and everywhere the delta was up in arms against the French. Belliard, with his 12,000 half-hearted men, had no real choice but to give in, especially when the British offered to transport the French army back to France.

The last scenes of the campaign were something of an anticlimax. On July 15, 1801, the French marched out of Cairo to the boats that were waiting at Bulaq to take them down to Rosetta, a strange procession: the soldiers and the servants, the women and what was left of the crestfallen speculators, the sick on litters, donkeys carrying the baggage and the plunder. Kléber's body, embalmed and coffined, was placed in a leading boat and a black flag flew overhead. By October 1801 the last French soldier had left Egyptian soil, and the British force that had ejected them soon followed them back to Europe.

It was a sad end to a great adventure, and it created the impression that Bonaparte had accomplished nothing very much in Egypt. The Suez Canal was not dug, the new boulevards and waterways in Cairo were abandoned, French military law was forgotten along with their new scheme of weights and measures, their hospitals, their census and their proposed dams along the river. As for Bonaparte's vision of conquering India and the Ottoman Empire, it had vanished as completely as Conté's colored balloon.

Yet this scarcely states the true case. Almost all Bonaparte's plans for the westernization of Egypt were eventually carried out—it was a Frenchman who built the Suez Canal half a century later—and the work of the Institute filled a gap in human knowledge that had persisted since Roman times. There is hardly an aspect of Egyptian life that is not carefully examined in the twenty-four volumes of their monumental *Description de l'Égypte*. It was one of the most ambitious publications ever attempted, an enormous guidebook that was used by every successive invader in the nineteenth century. Even its inaccuracies were provocative. This was a true census of Egypt. And when Champollion in the late 1820s began the science of Egyptology by deciphering the hieroglyphics on the Rosetta Stone, a way back into the past was opened up as well.[1]

But it was upon the future of the country that the French invasion had its chief effect. Like land on which oil is found, or like some large neglected property in the path of a new highway, Egypt had suddenly become an immensely valuable territory. It was no longer possible for the British to think of India as being tucked away safely at the end of the long route round the Cape: India could now be directly menaced from Egypt, and the Red Sea, instead of a forgotten backwater, had become a vital short-cut to Europe. From now on it was not feasible for the British to allow an enemy to remain in Egypt, and if they were unwilling to occupy the country themselves they were equally bound to keep the French out. Gradually, too, England was forced to enter the Red Sea, to patrol it with her warships, to establish bases on its shores, and to ensure that Ethiopia remained friendly. Thus all three countries watered by the Nile on its long journey from Lake Tana to the Mediterranean—Egypt, the Sudan and Ethiopia—were drawn into a new scheme

[1] The stone, now in the British Museum, was taken from Cairo to Alexandria and there surrendered to the British in 1801, but Bonaparte, before leaving Egypt, had caused impressions of the inscriptions to be taken, and it was from one of these copies that Champollion worked.

of international politics; and in the end, when Britain had failed to guarantee their neutrality by means of diplomacy, she inevitably went to war. Her eventual occupation, at first of Egypt, and then of the Sudan, and her invasion of Ethiopia, which is dealt with in the next chapter, were all the indirect result of Bonaparte's invasion.

CHAPTER NINE

THE EMPEROR THEODORE

THE idea that the Blue Nile might be blocked or poisoned at its source in Ethiopia as a means of destroying Egypt had been canvassed in every age. It was nonsense, of course. Even now all the genius of modern engineering could not divert the Nile from its course or prevent its annual flood, and the poisoning of such a vast amount of water is a childish dream of evil. But in the early 1860s nobody was at all sure of this. Nobody had followed the Blue Nile from Lake Tana to the Sudanese border; nobody even knew where the White Nile came from. And so the fortunes of Ethiopia were bound up in the fortunes of the river, and the struggle for the control of that country was largely a struggle for the control of the Blue Nile.

Work on the Suez Canal was now far advanced, and it was apparent to any sensible observer that the Red Sea route would soon abolish the need for the long voyage round the Cape. England could not possibly afford to have an enemy in control of Ethiopia and the Red Sea ports; she would be bound to intervene. In 1864 such an enemy appeared, the Emperor Theodore.

It has always been accepted that the Emperor Theodore was a mad dog let loose, and so he was in many ways, even by the savage standards of Ethiopia itself. Yet Theodore's appalling reputation does not fit him absolutely. A touch of nobility intervenes; he was far too emotional to be a calculating villain, and there was no real method in his madness. "His wrath," a contemporary said, "was terrible and all trembled." But then he was energetic and decisive, and he was also very religious, and very generous; nobody ever contested the fact that he had that sort of unthinking courage that comes to some people as naturally as the air they breathe.

He was sincere in the beginning; he really did try to abolish slavery, to pay his soldiers instead of allowing them to plunder. He believed right up to the moment of his death that he was destined to restore the glories of the ancient Ethiopian empire, and in that cause his personal and moral daring were boundless.

That was the trouble. He had no judgment and he never knew where to stop. When he was finally defeated in the long chaotic struggle to coerce, bludgeon, and bully his people out of the Middle Ages he turned, like an animal at bay, to senseless butchery. He was like a child who knows that he is doing wrong, yearns for forgiveness, for a way out, and finding none gives way entirely to his anger, hoping that it will create its own justification. Had he had anyone to help him in the terribly difficult business of adjusting himself without loss of dignity to the modern world it might have been a different story. But he was surrounded by ignorance and superstition, and a wilder, more barbaric place than Ethiopia in the nineteenth century cannot be imagined.

Theodore claimed that he was of royal blood and in the direct line of kings descending from Solomon and Alexander the Great. He was nothing of the sort. He was the son of a small local chieftain, and he had no connection with the royal line. He was a self-made king if there ever was one. He was born in 1818 in the border district of Kwara, close to the source of the Blue Nile in the Christian province of Amhara. Amhara was closely invested by Muhammadans—by the Turks, Egyptians, and Arabs in the deserts of the Sudan, and by the Galla tribes of central Ethiopia itself—and Theodore grew up knowing hardly anything but war against the Muslims. It is true that he had other quarrels as well, and could kill his brother Christians with a clear and determined conscience, but in the main he considered himself a crusader against the Muslims, and if we are to understand him this is an aspect of his character that one ought never to forget. From the earliest beginnings he seems to have been singled out as an exceptional man. He looked like a leader. He was black and very beautiful, a man with a high forehead, a lithe, athletic body, and there was a certain air of grandeur in his bearing. He was educated in a monastery, but very soon abandoned the priesthood to become a soldier: and in the ruthless arts of Ethiopian tribal warfare he was a master.

By 1853, when he was thirty-five, he had defeated all the rival chiefs on Lake Tana and had overrun Amhara. Next he turned with his little army to the neighboring provinces of Tigré, Gojam, and Shoa, and by 1855 most of the ruling families in those areas were either killed or in his hands. The Turks were still threatening him from the Red Sea coast and the Sudan, but in Ethiopia itself this new St. George was triumphant. Both Gondar and the great mountain fortress of Magdala had fallen to him, but he still preferred to move about the countryside in a vast tented camp with his court and his army around him. He now declared himself Theodore III, Emperor of Ethiopia, and it was a title which, for the moment, nobody could dispute. It was even thought worthwhile in England to appoint a consul, Walter G. Plowden, to conclude a treaty with him.

Plowden, at the time of his appointment, had already been in Ethiopia for a number of years, and had become an intimate of Theodore's, while his companion, an engineer named Bell, had even been appointed to act as a kind of grand chamberlain and secretary at the court. A number of missionaries, of German extraction but sponsored by British religious organizations, were also on the scene. By the late 1850s, therefore, things were going very well with England's policy of building up friends along the Red Sea route. But in 1860 disaster suddenly intervened: Plowden on one of his journeys through the country was killed by tribesmen near Gondar. Theodore at once marched with Bell against the culprits, and as a gesture of condolence to his dead English friend slaughtered and mutilated about two thousand of them—a holocaust exceptional even for Ethiopia. During the fighting Bell rushed to the assistance of Theodore and was killed.

It now became necessary for the British government to find a new representative at the emperor's court, and their choice fell on a Captain Charles Duncan Cameron of the Indian Service.

At first all was warmth and friendship. Cameron arrived at Gondar in 1862, and there presented Theodore with a brace of pistols, each with a silver plate on its stock inscribed with the words, "Presented to Theodore, Emperor of Abyssinia, by Victoria, Queen of Great Britain and Ireland, for his kindness to her servant Plowden, 1861." Whether or not Theodore took this to be a gracious acknowledgment of the massacre he had just carried out is not known, but it is certain that he was delighted by the gift, and Cameron suggested to Theodore that he should send envoys to England to conclude a new treaty of friendship with the Queen. Probably what Cameron intended was nothing more than a formal exchange of civilities, but Theodore took up the idea with all the seriousness of a petty African chieftain wishing to establish his importance in the great outer world. He drafted a letter to the Queen and directed Cameron to deliver it, probably thinking that Cameron would do so in person. Since this fatal letter was the source of all the misunderstandings and tragedies that were to follow it is worth quoting a translation from the Amharic:

> "In the name of the Father, of the Son, and of the Holy Ghost, one God in Trinity, chosen by God, King of Kings, Theodore of Ethiopia, to her Majesty Victoria, Queen of England.
>
> "I hope your Majesty is in good health. By the power of God I am well. My fathers, the Emperors, having forgotten the Creator, He handed over their kingdom to the Gallas and the Turks. But God created me, lifted me out of the dust, and restored this Empire to my rule. He endowed me with power and enabled me to stand in the place of my fathers. By this power I drove away the Gallas. As for the Turks I have told them to leave the land of my ancestors. They refuse. I am now going to wrestle with them.
>
> "Mr. Plowden and my late Grand Chamberlain, the Englishman Bell, used to tell me that there is a great

Christian Queen, who loves all Christians. When they said to me this: 'We are able to make you known to her and to establish friendship between you,' then in those times I was very glad. I gave them my love, thinking that I had found your Majesty's goodwill.

"All men are subject to death, and my enemies, thinking to injure me, killed these my friends. But by the power of God I have exterminated those enemies, not leaving one alive, though they were of my own family, that I may get, by the power of God, your friendship. I was prevented by the Turks occupying the seacoast from sending you an Embassy when I was in difficulty. Consul Cameron arrived with a letter and presents of friendship. By the power of God I was very glad hearing of your welfare and being assured of your amity. I have received your presents and thank you much.

"I fear that if I send ambassadors with presents of amity by Consul Cameron, they may be arrested by the Turks. And now I wish that you may arrange for the safe passage of my ambassadors everywhere on the road. I wish to have an answer to this letter by Consul Cameron, and that he may conduct my Embassy to England. See how Islam oppresses the Christian."

This letter eventually found its way to London, and in the normal course of events a polite, though possibly noncommittal answer would have been returned. But on this occasion someone in the Foreign Office slipped up: the letter was read, perhaps smiled at a little, and forgotten. To a man of Theodore's pride this was already an insult, and now the Foreign Office proceeded to injury: they sent Cameron an instruction to make his way down to Kassala in the Sudan, where, among other matters, he was to inquire into the prospects of growing cotton and to investigate the slave trade.

Now the Muslim Sudan was Theodore's bitter enemy, and the Turks were at that moment actively preparing to invade Ethiopia. No Ethiopian could visit the Sudan without being branded as a traitor. Undeterred by this Cameron set off, and it was only some months later that Theodore, who imagined he had gone down to the coast on his way to England, heard of his real destination. He flew into a rage. One cannot but sympathize with him a little; what was this Englishman doing, coming to him with professions of friendship, and then surreptitiously going off into the camp of his enemies? The absence of any answer to the letter was now explained: England was plotting a campaign against Ethiopia from the Sudan. Theodore had been brought up in a world of treachery and of quick revenge, and so now he naturally fell upon the European missionaries at Gondar. They were put into irons and held as hostages, and when Cameron returned in January 1864, all unsuspecting, from his mission, he too was thrown into prison. Explanations were useless. A savage hatred and a savage pride had been aroused, and in the extremity of one of his rages Theodore ordered Cameron to be tortured.

The news of these dealings reached Aden in April 1864, and in Aden the British Political Agent was a shrewd and energetic man named Colonel Merewether. He at once got through to London with an urgent request that Theodore's letter, now two years old, should be answered at once. The government was further prodded into action by *The Times* newspaper which published a communication that Cameron had smuggled out of his prison in Gondar. "There is no hope of my release," he wrote, "unless a letter is sent as an answer to His Majesty."

It was not an easy situation. The prisoners were held by a half-civilized chieftain well out of the range of British power or influence in the heart of Ethiopia, and a threatening reply might well mean their further torture or even death. Eventually a careful and mollifying document was drawn up addressed to "Our Good Friend Theodore, King of Abyssinia," and signed at Balmoral on May 26, 1864, "Victoria R." with the royal signet attached. It thanked Theodore for his good wishes, congratulated him on having established his authority in Ethiopia, and promised to receive an Ethiopian embassy in England. The pith of the letter, dealing with the release of Cameron, was as follows:

"Accounts have indeed reached Us of late that your Majesty had withdrawn your favor from Our servant. We trust, however, that these accounts have originated in false representations on the part of persons ill-disposed to your Majesty, and who may desire to produce an alteration in Our feelings towards you. But your Majesty can give no better proof of the sincerity of the sentiments which you profess towards Us, nor ensure more effectually a continuance of Our friendship and goodwill, than by dismissing Our servant Cameron, and any other Europeans who may desire it, from your Court, and by affording them every assistance and protection on their journey to the destination to which they desire to proceed."

A strange choice was made of an envoy to deliver this message. Hormuzd Rassam was not an Englishman by birth: he was an Iraki born in Mosul of Christian parents. As a young man he had studied at Oxford, and had eventually adopted British nationality. Some time before this he had found his way on to Merewether's staff in Aden. Perhaps it was thought in England that a wily Oriental would be the best man to handle Theodore, perhaps it was simply because Rassam was on the spot and Merewether supported him, but at all events this unusual agent was instructed to negotiate with Theodore on behalf of the British government, and he was soon to prove himself very able indeed. He was a supple and persistent man, not at all lacking in bravery. Two assistants were given him for his long and dangerous journey into the interior: a doctor named Henry Blanc, and later, a Lieutenant Prideaux of the Bombay army.

In July 1864 Rassam and his party were taken in a British gunboat from Aden to Massawa, which was then in Egyptian territory, and the customary gateway into Ethiopia. Even here the fear of Theodore was so great that many of the natives believed that he heard everything that was said about him even though he was hundreds of miles away, and Rassam was warned that he should on no account enter Ethiopia without the emperor's permission. He wrote a letter to Theodore saying that he was the bearer of a letter from Queen Victoria and asking, very politely, for this permission. With some difficulty he then obtained messengers who were willing to convey it to Gondar. Other letters and a sum of money were dispatched to Cameron, and Rassam sat down to wait.

It was a long wait indeed. All the rest of that year went by in the fetid and plague-ridden port of Massawa with no word from the interior, and it was not until early in 1865 that Rassam began to get messages from the captives. Cameron wrote that some twenty or thirty Europeans and their families had been rounded up, some like the missionaries Mr. and Mrs. Flad being with Theodore in the field near Lake Tana, and in relative freedom, while others like himself and the missionaries Rosenthal and Stern were now in Magdala and chained in such a way that it was difficult to stand upright. Rassam had written a second letter to Theodore in October 1864, but to this there was still no reply. A third letter, even politer in tone, was now sent off and remained unanswered. Cameron, who now began corresponding fairly freely from Magdala, suggested that Rassam might perhaps try a stronger tone. He added, "But, for God's sake, do not come up here; he will cage you as sure as a gun, as he thinks that while he has us in his hands he is safe from attack, and, of course, with a swell like you in addition, matters would only be better for him. . . ."

At last in August 1865, more than a year after Rassam's arrival at Massawa, word was received that Cameron had been released from his chains, and this news was followed by a letter from Theodore himself. Most of it was a self-righteous and petulant outburst against the British Consul, but there was a gleam of hope in the last paragraph: "Be it known to Hormuzd Rassam that there exists just now a rebellion in Tigré. By the power of God, come round by way of Metemma. When you reach Metemma, send me a messenger, and, by the power of God, I will send people to receive you."

There were difficulties here. Metemma lay hundreds of miles away in the Sudan, south of Kassala, where the wet season had begun, spreading disease and making all travel impossible.

Rassam, who preferred on this and on all other occasions the soft tone, replied: "Most Gracious Sovereign. I . . . beg to inform your Majesty that, in consequence of the prevailing sickness at Kassala and the neighborhood, I dare not for the present come up to you via Metemma, as you have directed"; instead he would go up to Cairo and there await the ending of the wet season in October.

Rassam had a twofold motive in going first to Cairo; he wanted to get fresh instructions from London by telegraph, and he wanted to buy suitable presents to carry in to Theodore. The presents at least were easy enough to obtain in the Cairo bazaars, and an exotic lot they were: several chandeliers, mirrors and glassware, two cases of liqueur and a mass of general stores.

The first news he received when he returned to Massawa was that Cameron and his fellow captives, far from being released from their chains, were more heavily bound than ever. Rassam and his party now lost no further time, and on October 16, 1865, they set off from Massawa in the midst of a cholera epidemic, the chandeliers and other baggage securely lashed to a string of camels. They had six hundred and twenty miles to go, much of it over country that had barely been explored or mapped. On November 21 they arrived at Metemma. Here they were inside Ethiopian territory for the first time, and on the track that led up to Lake Tana, only one hundred miles away. Rassam hastened to send off messengers to Theodore announcing his arrival. After a week's delay a note came in from Cameron, urging haste. "The King," he wrote, "sent us a cow a-piece sometime back—the first notice he has taken of us since the torturing. He has spoken rather kindly about us lately in public. But we are still chained hand and foot."

This was followed by an effusive letter from Theodore himself, calling Rassam his "beloved" and saying that an escort was on its way to him. On December 28 the British party set off into the cold of the mountains and was duly met by the escort—a horde of fourteen hundred men—close to the western shores of Lake Tana. They were nearing their goal at last.

Years afterwards Rassam wrote an account of this journey, and in a remarkable way it reads like an exact repetition of Bruce. Here it all is once more, the unchanging black Biblical world of Ethiopia: the raw-beef banquets, the swarms of tribesmen in their white robes trailing across the landscape, the villages ruined by war, the gaunt prophet-like figures of the Coptic priests emerging from their round hut-churches, the childish posturing of the officials, the abject fear of the king, the tej drinking, the flowers and the honey, the lions roaring at night, the vast horizons of mountains, the bigotry and violence of the Middle Ages in surroundings of fantastic natural beauty; nothing had altered.

For some days they marched on, rounding Lake Tana on the west, and finally on January 26, 1866, they reached the source of the Little Abbai—the Little Blue Nile—where Bruce had had his great moment of discovery a hundred years before. Perching on a green hilltop close by was Theodore's camp, his own great white tent in the center and surrounding it on every side thousands of other smaller tents and makeshift huts.

Theodore sent a warm message to his guests to advance, and Rassam was presented with a mule upon which he was to make his ceremonial entry into the camp. Hastily he got into his "blue political suit," while Blanc and Prideaux changed into scarlet jackets, and as they went forward they were met by Aito Samuel, the emperor's chamberlain, and officials of the court. The escort, now swollen to ten thousand men, fired off a ragged salute as they passed the first tents. Rassam was much moved. "After dragging out a miserable existence for eighteen weary months," he writes, "in an unhealthy climate and among semi-barbarous races . . . in vain efforts to reach the most impracticable man that ever swayed a scepter . . . here we were at last, about to obtain the long desired audience."

A red tent had been erected for the occasion, and here Theodore received them, sitting on a sofa, his long robe muffling up his face and his courtiers in a circle round him. Rassam opened the proceedings by producing his famous letter from Victoria, now eighteen months old, but Theodore did not read it at once. Instead he launched into a long and involved harangue about his grievances. Speaking in Amharic through an interpreter, he declared that Cameron had behaved very badly, that the missionaries had slandered him, that he was surrounded by treachery even among his own followers.

Next morning there was a second interview. Rassam was informed that orders had gone to Magdala for the release of the captives, and Theodore handed him a reply to Victoria's letter. It was a strange document. In it Theodore described himself as "an ignorant Ethiopian," and he asked the Queen's pardon: "Counsel me but do not blame me, O Queen. . . ." But once again he could not prevent himself from reverting to his grievances, and Rassam was forced to listen to another long outburst of complaint.

Choosing his moment, Rassam presented his chandeliers. They were well received and the second interview closed.

So far so good. But the British were soon to discover that things do not move quickly in Ethiopia. It was announced that the capital was to be transported into the Damot province, where Theodore intended to demolish some tribes he suspected of rebellion. Rassam and his party were to accompany the march as far as Lake Tana, and were then to go off to the village of Korata on the southeastern shore. Here they were to await the arrival of the prisoners from Magdala.

The march was an astonishing affair. Each day some ninety thousand people, men, women, children, and their herds of sheep and cattle, got on the move, straggling over the hills and valleys like some enormous crawling dragon. Theodore led the way, and he showed great skill in keeping order among his rabble. Starting each morning at seven they sometimes covered as much as thirty miles in a day, and they kept this up for a week on end. At every ravine and difficult river crossing Theodore turned back to see his followers across, often himself lending a hand with the older women and children. Each night a city of twenty thousand tents and huts sprang up in an instant. Each day skirmishing parties of warriors replenished supplies by pillaging and despoiling the wayside villages.

The British party was given a place of honor in the van of the march, and Theodore was almost embarrassingly attentive to Rassam. At their first camp on the Little Abbai Rassam slipped and nearly fell into the stream. Theodore rushed forward and grasped his arm. "Cheer up," he said, helping Rassam up the bank, "don't be afraid." Each day there was a gift: an antelope which Theodore had shot, a brace of partridges, a battery of firearms, a message saying that all the expenses of the British party while they were in Ethiopia would be met by the royal treasury.

Close to the lake, on February 6, they parted, Theodore going south to continue his marauding, while the British, attended by Samuel and a strong escort, crossed in boats to the opposite shore. Within a few days Rassam had a message from Theodore saying that he had set up his own camp at Zagé, close to the mouth of the Little Abbai, on the opposite shore of the lake—Rassam could actually see the smoke rising from the camp-fires—and giving an assurance that an escort had gone off to Magdala to collect the captives. The letter was accompanied by the gift of two lion cubs.

By now Rassam had begun to form a fairly clear idea of the nature of the people he had come to rescue. They appeared to number about thirty adults in all, British, French, German, Swiss, and their Ethiopian wives, and twenty-three children, and they were divided into three groups. First there was a team of seven skilled European workmen, Germans for the most part, who had enlisted in Theodore's service and were not, properly speaking, prisoners at all, since they moved freely about the emperor's camp. Then there were the German missionaries, Mr. and Mrs. Flad and their three children, together with four more Germans; and finally there were the people Theodore hated most—Cameron and his European staff of four, and the German missionaries, Mr. and Mrs. Stern and Mr. and Mrs. Rosenthal. All these last were in Magdala, and presumably had just been released from their fetters.

One might have supposed that the European colony clung very much together in these dangerous and violent surroundings, but this, Rassam now learned, was very far from being the case; there were constant dissensions and animosities among some of them.

For the moment, however, there was nothing for Rassam to do but to wait, to shoot hippopotamuses in the lake and to reply to the stream of flowery messages which Theodore kept dispatching daily from Zagé. Was his beloved friend Rassam happy and contented? Had he everything he wanted? Was he in good health? Yes, Rassam was well enough, but he had the uneasy feeling that things were not quite right, that Theodore was a dangerous man to deal with, and that in some unforeseen way the situation could change in an instant. The present gust of excessive friendship was a little too good to last.

Towards the end of February the missionary Flad arrived at Korata, and immediately confirmed these suspicions. He warned Rassam to use great caution and to take nothing for granted as yet. For the moment, however, the signs were favorable. Early in March the artisans came across to the British camp, and they were soon followed by their wives. Then on March 10 there was a moving moment when Cameron, haggard with weakness after two years in chains, arrived with the Magdala party and the remainder of Flad's group from Debra Tabor—eighteen of them in all. Rassam deliberately received Cameron rather formally, since he was Theodore's especial enemy, and any great show of warmth towards him might appear to Theodore as bad faith. The European colony was now united at Korata, and all that remained was for the emperor to give the word for them to go.

That word did not arrive. Instead a message of a very different kind was delivered: Theodore demanded that Rassam should hold an inquiry into the misdeeds of Cameron and his companions and let him know the result. A long, confused and wholly bogus list of charges against the captives was given to Rassam to assist him in his inquiry. It was the first hint of the danger ahead, and Rassam, consulting with the others, agreed that it would be foolhardy to oppose Theodore at this moment. After all, they were hundreds of miles from civilization and absolutely helpless in the hands of a man they believed mad. Theodore wanted justification for what he had done before he would let them go, and the only sensible thing to do was to let him have it.

Rassam publicly read out the charges in his tent, went through the form of listening to evidence, and then concocted a solemn letter to Theodore saying that "all confessed that they had done wrong" and asked forgiveness.

It seemed for the moment that this concession was all that Theodore required. Rassam, Blanc and Prideaux were summoned to Zagé to say good-bye, and they crossed the lake on rafts, changing into their uniforms when they landed. Zagé, then as now, was a wooded promontory jutting out into the lake and famous for its coffee and its pythons (two of them about this time were presented by Theodore to Rassam), and here the royal camp was established a little back from the shore. The British party was received with every show of friendliness; Theodore was waiting for them outside his tent and taking Rassam by the hand he led him into the audience-hall. Here they talked amiably for a while, and Theodore with pride displayed the two pistols that Plowden had brought him from Victoria. Yet there was a certain uneasiness in the background, and next day, while they waited in their tents, the British party heard that Theodore had summoned all his chiefs to decide whether or not the captives should be allowed to go. The chiefs apparently were in favor of it, but Theodore kept insisting that he must have some guarantee that once across the border they would not malign him. Still with nothing decided, the British were sent back to Korata the following day.

At length, in early April, Theodore brought himself to a decision: the prisoners could go, making their way out of Ethiopia on the Gondar route, and Rassam, Blanc and Prideaux were to come to Zagé to make their last farewells. On Friday, April 13, the two parties set off, Cameron and his people heading north towards the border, and the three members of the mission once more crossing Lake Tana to Zagé.

This time there was no friendly reception for Rassam on the

shore. Instead they heard that Theodore had passed the last three days in a drunken debauch, and that now they were to proceed to the audience-hall. On entering they saw no sign of Theodore, but the place was crowded with the leading men about the court. "Suddenly," says Rassam, "three strapping chiefs fell on me, two of whom held my arms and the other the tail of my coat . . . and, on looking behind for my companions, I found that they also had been arrested and were being roughly handled by the soldiers."

It was now revealed that Theodore was sitting listening behind the door a few feet away, and that the audience-hall had been converted into a court. Charges were read out: Rassam had sent the prisoners away without first reconciling them to the emperor, he had sent letters to the coast without permission —the rigmarole went on and on, and Rassam's every attempt to deny and explain was pushed aside. Cameron and his party had also been arrested on the other side of the lake and were now being brought into Zagé.

On the following day all the prisoners were put on trial together. The meeting was held in the open under a hot sun with a thousand Ethiopians in attendance, and Theodore sitting on a sofa in the center. He announced that one of the missionaries, Flad, was to be dispatched at once as an emissary to England. A secretary was sent for, and Theodore dictated a letter to Victoria saying that Cameron and the other prisoners would be allowed to go but that Rassam must remain behind. In a second letter Theodore asked that the Queen should send him a party of skilled workmen to help him modernize his country. Both letters were handed to Flad and he was sent off under escort (but without Mrs. Flad) down the track to Metemma. Rassam and the remainder of the prisoners, well knowing that none of them would be released until Flad returned with a reply—if even then—were marched back to their quarters.

The cat-and-mouse game now captivated Theodore entirely. Most of the prisoners were allowed to walk freely about the camp, and a shower of fresh presents descended upon Rassam and his two assistants, Blanc and Prideaux: saddles inlaid with gold, a special medal "The Cross and Solomon's Seal," and elaborate silk shirts, the particular sign of the emperor's favor. April 24 was Victoria's birthday, and on hearing this Theodore ordered a twenty-one-gun salute and a feast of raw meat. Hoping further to amuse his guests he took them on hunting expeditions along the lake, and one day organized a joust in which he himself, riding furiously, was a leading performer. Meanwhile it was all too painfully evident to the prisoners from the cries they heard by day and night that others of his victims, Ethiopians who had fallen out of favor, were being flogged and tortured to death.

Then, with the beginning of the rains in June, cholera broke out. When a hundred men were dying every day Theodore ordered a general move around the southern end of the lake. On June 7 the whole army with the prisoners in its midst crossed the Blue Nile just below its outlet from the lake and marched on to Rassam's old headquarters at Korata. But still the disease continued to spread, and they went on eastwards towards the higher ground around Debra Tabor, about thirty miles from the unhealthy lake. Here the prisoners were taken to quarters at Gaffat about three miles outside the town. Theodore himself laid the carpets in Rassam's house, and set up his own throne there so that the place would look like a royal residence.

Bewildered, humoring him, calculating every word before he uttered it, Rassam passively went on playing his part as a favorite dog who is alternatively patted and kicked by his master. But things could not continue at this pitch of half-hysterical make-believe for much longer. The prisoners were suddenly brought in from Gaffat and thrust into dark rooms in Debra Tabor. Theodore came to visit them in the middle of the night carrying a lantern and a jug of tej to drink to their friendship. "I used to hear that I was called a madman for my acts," he said to Rassam, "but I never believed it; now however, after my conduct towards you this afternoon, I have come to the conclusion that I am really so. But as Christians we ought always to be ready to forgive each other.'

This was the last time Rassam spoke to Theodore for a year and nine months. The emperor vanished with his army into the wilderness of the Ethiopian plateau, murdering, torturing, and laying waste the country as he went along. Left behind in the pouring rain at Debra Tabor the prisoners sat, like shipwrecked sailors, in their dismal jail awaiting rescue from the outside world.

CHAPTER TEN

PRISONERS OF THE EMPEROR

FLAD reached England in July 1866. A group of skilled workmen was enlisted, and he was instructed to take them back to Ethiopia together with some suitable gifts and a letter from Victoria to Theodore. He was to make sure, however, that Theodore released the prisoners before the workmen or the gifts were handed over. One rather wonders who these skilled workmen were that they should be so willing to put themselves in the lion's mouth, but apparently they were readily obtained.

The letter that Victoria signed at Balmoral on October 4, 1866, was a nice blending of persuasion and dignified reproof. She still addressed Theodore as "Our Good Friend," she indicated that she had received Flad and heard his news, and she added: "We will not disguise from your Majesty that we found it difficult to reconcile your assurances with the obstacles which were still opposed to the departure of our servants and the other Europeans from your country but . . . we gave our sanction to the engagement of your Majesty's service of skilled workmen, such as you desired to employ in Abyssinia.

"In full confidence that the cloud which has darkened the friendship of our relations will pass away on the return of Flad, and desiring that you should as soon as possible thereafter receive the articles which we had proposed to send your Majesty in token of our friendship, we have given orders that those articles should be forthwith sent to Massawa, to be delivered, for conveyance to your Majesty's court, to the officers whom you may depute to conduct our servant Rassam, and our servant Cameron, and the other Europeans, so far on their way to our presence. And so we bid you heartily farewell."

There it was then, the tactful bribe with just a hint of a threat behind it; let Theodore send his prisoners down to the Red Sea coast and he would have his workmen and his gifts, and no harm done.

Flad set off from England in October 1866, and reached Ethiopia in December. Theodore received him at once and was delighted with the letter, but he saw quite clearly what the game was. He did not send a reply but wrote instead to Rassam in prison. "I wish you to get the workmen sent up via Metemma, in order that they may teach me wisdom, and show me clever arts. When this is done, I shall make you glad, and send you away, by the power of God."

"To have refused the King's request," Rassam says, "would have placed all our lives in jeopardy," and so he sent off a letter to Stanley[1] asking him to agree to Theodore's request. Long before the letter reached England, however, Stanley had decided that it was impossible to bargain any further with Theodore for the moment and the workmen were sent home.

It was one of those dilemmas which are the agony of responsibility. What was the British government to do? They were unwilling to invade, threats were dangerous and negotiation was leading nowhere. The only alternative was to do nothing and hope that the situation would resolve itself, and this in the end was the policy into which the government drifted. All the spring and early summer of 1867 went by, and in England the Ethiopian affair, like a recurring bad dream, was dissolved in the more pressing events of the day. After all, Ethiopia was very far away.

Meanwhile, Theodore was free to continue with his morbid threatening and tormenting of the prisoners. Early in July 1866 they had been moved under a guard of a hundred men from Debra Tabor to Magdala, some ninety miles away to the east. Cameron and his staff had already been imprisoned there for two years, and now they endured all the weariness and hopelessness of dragging themselves back to their old quarters on the great rock where they had already suffered so much. There was worse to follow. At Magdala fetters were hammered on to their

[1] Lord Edward Stanley, in the Foreign Office.

legs once more, and this time Rassam, Blanc, and Prideaux were also chained. There was no real hope of escape: Magdala was a natural stronghold standing high about the Bascillo River where it runs down to the Blue Nile in central Ethiopia. It was the plug of an extinct volcano, and its plateau of basalt, three-quarters of a mile long by about half a mile wide, was perched a thousand feet above the surrounding plain. There was only one practical path up the precipitous sides of the mountain, and it was blocked at the entrance to the citadel by a formidable gate. Even if the prisoners managed to free themselves from their fetters, even if they obtained scaling ladders or forced the gate, they were still hundreds of miles away from civilization in a country that lived in abject fear of Theodore. It might have been possible for one or two of them to have got away—and indeed Rassam was offered the chance—but then reprisals would certainly have been taken on those left behind, and in any case it was quite impracticable to think that so large a party with so many women and small children in it could make its own unaided way out of Ethiopia.

And so they gave up thoughts of escape and made the best of things. Rassam, with a certain fatalism, says that apart from the fetters, none of them could really complain; much the worst part was the mental anxiety that at any moment they could be tortured or flung to death over the precipice, a form of execution Theodore had been fond of using in the past and was to use again. Physically they did rather well. They were accommodated in a group of huts close to the gate, and although these huts were made of branches and straw roofing, and water seeped through the bare floor in the wet season, they were soon made reasonably comfortable. Each hut was furnished with chairs, beds and a table, and had its fireplace in the center of the floor. The prisoners still possessed their Ethiopian servants and their baggage and European stores, and they were well fed; it was nothing exceptional for them to sit down to a dinner of soup, fish, two or three entrées, a joint, pudding, anchovy-toast or cream cheese. Tej, the Ethiopian mead, arak and coffee were obtainable, they made their own bread, and with seeds sent up from the coast by Merewether grew vegetables, which at this height and so near the equator developed to a fantastic size: peas five feet high, monstrous potatoes, and tomatoes that bore fruit all round the year. Rassam attracted myriads of the brilliant Ethiopian birds to his garden.

Magdala all through this time was being built up by Theodore as his principal capital, even though it was in the midst of the territory of the Muslim Gallas, his mortal enemies. It consisted of no more than two or three thousand huts scattered about the plateau, but it had its palace, its round church and a substantial house containing the royal treasure.

From the end of 1866 onwards Theodore was less concerned with the government of the Ethiopians than with their extermination. In November of that year he fell on the old capital of Gondar, where some rebels were holding out, and destroyed it utterly, even its Christian churches. Mass killings, the burning of people alive by hundreds, became a commonplace, and the whole of the valley of the Upper Blue Nile was a scene of brutality and terror that not even Bruce, or perhaps anyone in these regions, had ever witnessed. And the more Theodore slaughtered the more rebellions rose up against him. Up to now the bulk of his army, numbering about 100,000, had remained loyal, mainly through the habit of dumb and terrified obedience, but by 1867 desertions had begun and the ranks were diminishing rapidly. The province of Tigré, under a chieftain named Kassai, broke away entirely. Once for seven weeks Theodore was cut off from Magdala itself.

Rassam, corresponding regularly with Merewether in Aden and the three main rebel chiefs, was well aware of all these upheavals, and in July 1867 Merewether was able to give him a little hope; in England public opinion was beginning to stir itself at last, and the government was coming around to the notion that it was bound to rescue the prisoners if British prestige was to continue to mean anything in Africa and the Near East. In August a peremptory letter was sent to Theodore demanding the release of the prisoners forthwith, and when it remained unanswered orders were given for war.

There has never been in modern times a colonial campaign quite like the British expedition to Ethiopia in 1868. It was a fearsome undertaking; for hundreds of years the country had never been invaded, and the savage nature of the terrain alone was enough to promise failure. Unlike Bonaparte's expedition to Egypt, there was no secrecy whatever about this campaign, everyone knew all about it for months in advance, where it was going, what it proposed to do. It was debated at great length in the press, and although there was general sympathy for the prisoners many people in England were by no means enthusiastic about it. How was the army to get itself across the four-thousand-foot ravines in a country where there were no bridges, no roads, no modern appliances of any kind? Who could say that Theodore would not murder the prisoners out of hand once he heard the British had landed? Terrible dangers faced the soldiers; they would be exposed to unknown tropical diseases, adders would get into their blankets at night and fierce wild animals would attack them by day, they would die of thirst, they would die of frostbite, all their mules would succumb to the tsetse fly. One letter of protest followed another in the newspapers, and the insurance companies made a sharp increase in the rates applying to any man who took part in the expedition.

Wisely the government decided that if it was to go into this adventure at all things would have to be done with great thoroughness, whatever the expense. Control of the operations was confided to the Indian Army, since it was experienced in frontier warfare and could be transported without too much difficulty to the Red Sea, and the officer chosen to take command was one of the most promising soldiers of the day. Field-Marshal Lord Napier, whose statue looks down at us in Queen's Gate in London with such a grand air of distant horizons, may seem to the present generation a slightly comic figure, one of the spit-and-polish, up-and-at-'em school of Victorian generals. He was, however, a great deal more than this. That battered face contains a strong suggestion of humor and intelligence. "What do you think the Chinese in their *lingua franca* call the English Bishop?" he once wrote home from China. "No. 1

Heaven Pigeon: pigeon being the general name for business of all kinds." By the same token Napier himself might fairly have been described as No. 1 Army Pigeon. More than almost any other British soldier of his time he lived by war, but he did not come to it in the usual way. He was an engineer who for nearly twenty years had toiled up and down India building roads, canals, bridges and encampments before he was given a chance to show what he could do in an active command. When he did enter battle, however, he went in headlong, and twice had his horse shot from under him; and he made no fuss about his wounds. It was the Indian mutiny that made him. He directed the defense of Lucknow until its second relief, and from there he went on to take command of the British expedition that went to China and entered Peking in 1860. On his return to India he was given command of the Bombay Army, which was now directed to Ethiopia. He was at this time fifty-seven years of age, and he had recently married, on the death of his first wife, an eighteen-year-old English girl.

The methods by which Napier went about directing the huge machine that was now placed under his control were extremely sensible. First, intelligence officers were set to work examining all the records and maps of European explorers in Ethiopia from the time of Bruce onwards. Then while Merewether went off on a reconnaissance along the Red Sea coast to find a landing place, agents were sent inland to contact the rebel tribes.

By mid-August 1867 Napier was able to give the government his estimate of what was required: about 12,000 fighting men with roughly twice as many followers, at least 20,000 mules and other transport animals, artillery of all kinds including heavy mountain guns, and a fleet of 280 ships, both sail and steam, to carry the force to its destination. It was calculated that if the campaign were begun at the start of the dry season in December it could be completed by the following June—about six months in all.

Seventy years had now elapsed since Bonaparte's invasion of Egypt, and it is interesting to see the changes in the art of war.

The railway, the steamship and the telegraph, all of them unknown in Bonaparte's time, had now immensely extended the speed and scope of operations, and the range and power of guns had given the battlefield a new dimension. And yet there had been a slowing-down process as well: ten times the amount of equipment was required by a modern army in the field, and it had become immensely complicated. In the French invasion of Egypt nearly every soldier fought; now at least a dozen noncombatants were needed to support just one man at the front. At the same time warfare had grown much less dangerous: mass killings like those at Waterloo had vanished from the world and were not to reappear until the senseless trench fighting on the western front in 1914.

The infantry square was still used and so were the brightly colored uniforms which made such an admirable target on the battlefield. But the army's food was better, the medical services had changed out of recognition, the drill was more efficient, and the soldier was much less of an adventurer and more of a trained professional than he had ever been before.

The thoroughness and imagination with which this operation was planned are simply staggering. There can hardly have been more paper work done upon the landing of the Allied armies in Normandy in the last world war. It is the intelligence of these arrangements—the intricate dovetailing of things that were astonishingly modern with others that were hopelessly antique—that is so impressive. Thus, for example, forty-four trained elephants were to be sent from India to carry the heavy guns on the march, while hiring commissions were dispatched all over the Mediterranean and the Near East to obtain mules and camels to handle the lighter gear. A railway, complete with locomotives and some twenty miles of track, was to be laid across the coastal plain, and at the landing place large piers, lighthouses, and warehouses were to be established. Two condensers to convert salt seawater into fresh were needed, and a telegraph line several hundred miles in length was to maintain communication between the front and the base on the coast. Three hospital ships were to be equipped with ice-making machines, and among their stock of medicines were 250 dozen of port wine for each vessel. Then there was the question of the Maria Theresa dollars, the only general currency in Ethiopia. Not any dollar would do; only the 1780 minting was acceptable, and a search of the banks and moneylenders in Marseilles, Cairo and Vienna revealed that not nearly enough were available. A contract therefore had to be signed with the imperial mint in Vienna for a new issue of 500,000.

Each white soldier was to have two pairs of boots, an Indian helmet, a flannel cholera belt and a pair of gloves, and the force was to be followed into the field by a horde of native servants, at least two for every officer, one for himself and another for his horse. The rates of pay descended from Napier's 5,833 rupees a month (about $1,600) to the native soldier's 8½ rupees (about $2.40). Chaplains got $140 a month and elephant mahouts $2.80.

The food situation was greatly complicated by the fact that so many of the men came from different races and sects, each with its own series of taboos, but a basic store was laid down of compressed vegetables, dried milk, 50,000 tons each of salt beef and pork and 30,000 gallons of rum.

The force was to be divided into two divisions, each under the command of an experienced Indian Army campaigner. The British Museum sent a representative, Richard Holmes, who was to carry out archaeological excavations and to bid for the more worthwhile loot which, it was hoped, would be captured in Ethiopia—manuscripts, carvings and the like. A geographer and a zoologist were also added to the strength, and observers were sent by the French, Prussian, Italian, Dutch, Austrian and Spanish armies. Among the war correspondents were Henry Morton Stanley of the *New York Herald*, who was now on the threshold of his tremendous African career, and G. A. Henty, the author of the adventure stories, who represented the London *Standard*.

In the end, as always happens in every expedition, Napier found that he had underestimated the number of men he required. He finished up with 32,000 men (which included only

13,000 soldiers, of whom 4,000 were Europeans and 9,000 natives), and 55,000 animals. But then this was a most unusual sort of campaign, a struggle against the physical nature of the country rather than against an enemy, a long march rather than a battle, and no naval man could fail to approve of the professionalism with which the whole vast, complicated organization was put into motion. From Calcutta and Bombay, from Liverpool and London, sailing ships and paddle-steamers, vessels that were a combination of steam and sail, converged upon the Red Sea at their appointed times. Over a million dollars was spent in hiring these ships from private firms, and they carried on board every possible contrivance to set up a new temporary civilization in the wilderness, for Napier expected, rightly, that he would find nothing in Ethiopia. The elephant squad alone, a minor piece in the immense jigsaw, required two transports to be specially fitted up. The animals were slung on board without mishap at Bombay and placed in holds with a temporary flooring of stones and shingle. They stood back to back with their heads towards the sides, and a corridor between them to allow the attendants to pass to and fro. A seasick elephant was a formidable thing, and in the Calcutta moorings they had to face a cyclone.

Early in October 1867 Merewether returned from his reconnaissance and reported that he had fixed on Zula as a landing place. This was a derelict village standing on an open plain in Annesley Bay, about thirty miles south of Massawa, in Egyptian territory—and the Muslim Egyptians were ready to give all the help they could in a campaign against their ancient Christian enemies in Ethiopia. The landing therefore would be unopposed. Once the army had crossed the narrow coastal plain they would be faced with a very steep rough climb to the Ethiopian plateau eight thousand feet above, and even more difficult and dangerous passes lay beyond. But there was no avoiding these obstacles; this was the nature of Ethiopia and the explanation why she had never before been invaded as thoroughly as she was to be invaded now. All reports from the interior indicated that Theodore, beset by rebellions, would not contest the British march inland, but would make a stand at Magdala where the prisoners were held, and Magdala was therefore set as the first general objective of the expedition. It lay just under four hundred miles from the coast.

In mid-October 1867, the first advance guard, mainly engineers, arrived at Zula and began to construct a port. By the end of the month a first pier, seven hundred yards long, was completed, with a tramway laid along it, and ships and barges were arriving on every tide to discharge their men, animals, and stores. A hutted and tented town had sprung up in the billowing dust along the shore and every day it expanded. A labor force of many thousands of Indians, Persians, Egyptians and Ethiopians toiled back and forth between the ships and the shore. By the first week in December a second pier, nine hundred feet long and thirty feet wide, was finished, the railway was being pushed inland and Zula had become a city; it had its native bazaar, its hospitals and storehouses and its huge compounds for the animals and their drivers. The two condensers fixed at the end of the piers were producing one hundred and sixty tons of fresh water a day to add to the million tons brought over from Aden.

It was all most impressive, but it contained elements of chaos too. An unknown and unidentified fever had broken out among the horses and mules, and they were dying in hundreds every day. Many of the animals that survived had been landed without attendants, or tethering ropes, and these roamed over the barren plain in search of water. But there was no water. In the appalling heat every well that Merewether had discovered in October went dry, and neither the condensers nor the incoming ships could keep up sufficient supplies to cope with the reinforcements of men and animals that were arriving every day. Frantic mobs of native workers gathered around the water points each night when the ration was doled out, and wildcat strikes were breaking out among the unloading parties. In the anchorage the shipping was getting itself into a serious tangle, and some vessels were left for days or even weeks before they could find a berth. Zula with its perpetual swarms of flies, its fearful heat, its resentful labor gangs, and its dead and dying animals was a dismal place.

However, things were going rather better at the front where Merewether and the advance guard had pushed inland to a place called Senafé some forty miles from the sea. They had met no opposition from the inhabitants, but on their way up to the plateau along the dried-up bed of the Kumayli River they had encountered tremendous obstacles. On the Suru Pass, where the Ethiopian plateau rose up in a series of immense precipices, the track was barely twenty feet wide and strewn with boulders, and engineers were now at work there blasting and ramping a way through to enable the elephants, gun-carriages and carts to follow on. At Senafé itself all was transformed. Great forests of euphorbia, juniper and acacias spread away, water was fresh and abundant, and the temperature fell near freezing point at night. Both men and animals instantly revived once they reached these heights.

Merewether was already in friendly correspondence with Kassai, the rebel leader of Tigré, through whose territory the army was to pass, and messages had come in from the prisoners at Magdala saying that they were all well.

Napier's proclamation to the people of Ethiopia was issued about this time:

"To the Governors, the Chiefs, the Religious Orders, and the people of Abyssinia.

"It is known to you that Theodorus King of Abyssinia detains in captivity the British Consul Cameron, the British Envoy Rassam, and many others, in violation of the laws of all civilized nations. All friendly persuasion having failed to obtain their release, my Sovereign has commanded me to lead an army to liberate them.

"All who befriend the prisoners or assist in their liberation shall be rewarded, but those who may injure them shall be severely punished.

"When the time shall arrive for the march of a British Army through your country, bear in mind, people of

Abyssinia, that the Queen of England has no unfriendly feeling towards you, and no design against your country or your liberty. Your religious establishments, your persons and your property shall be carefully protected. All supplies required for my soldiers shall be paid for; no peaceable inhabitants shall be molested.

"The sole object for which the British force has been sent to Abyssinia is the liberation of Her Majesty's servants and others unjustly detained as captives, and as soon as that object is effected it will be withdrawn. There is no intention to occupy permanently any portion of the Abyssinian territory, or to interfere with the Government of the country."

The reconnaissance party now pushed on another thirty-seven miles beyond Senafé to the town of Adigrat in the heart of Kassai's country, and about a quarter of the way to Magdala. They were met everywhere with friendliness, or at any rate with passivity, and there was still no sign of Theodore or his army.

On the coast meanwhile the situation had greatly improved with the arrival of General Staveley, the second-in-command. He provided Zula with a central strong control which had been lacking before since most of the senior officers had gone inland in the wake of the advance guard. Little by little the unloading program was sorted out, the town reorganized and cleaned up, and the incoming soldiers were marched off towards the front as they came ashore. By the end of the year most of the fighting force had arrived, and the engineers had succeeded in opening up a rough cart-track all the way to Senafé on the heights above.

On January 2, 1868, Napier himself arrived from Bombay in the steam frigate *Octavia*, with his staff. He disembarked, says the official history, "in some state." The *Octavia* fired off all her guns and was given an answering salute from a mountain battery on shore. A guard of redcoats was drawn up on the wharf and the natives of Zula were treated to the strange and wonderful spectacle of a British brass band giving of its best amidst the swirling dust. The commander in chief was followed ashore by the first nineteen elephants, and the remaining twenty-five arrived soon afterwards, all of them eating well and apparently ready for the fray ahead. They were possibly the first Indian elephants seen in Africa since the time of Alexander the Great.

Napier ordered an immediate acceleration of the program of road and bridge building, of the digging of wells and the extension of the wharves, and then turned to the organization of his striking force. A picked force of five thousand men was to make the final dash to Magdala, while the remainder were to guard the lines of communication to the coast. In order to relieve the burden on the long antlike stream of mules and camels now on the march into the interior, instructions were given for all personal baggage to be cut down. Three officers henceforward were to share a bell tent and to make do with one mule each for their baggage, and with one mess-servant, one batman and one grass-cutter between them.

For three weeks Napier worked in Zula putting the final touches to his plans. Then on January 25 he went up to the pleasant heights of Senafé to take command in person. On this same day the expedition suffered its first casualty: a Colonel Dunn, V.C., was accidentally killed whilst shooting partridges in the hills.

CHAPTER ELEVEN

THE MARCH TO MAGDALA

THEODORE first heard of the approach of the British in early December 1867, and he professed to be delighted. "I long for the day," he said to some of his German workmen, "when I shall see a disciplined European army," and he went on to speak of a legend that a great Ethiopian king and a great European king were destined to meet in Ethiopia and decide the country's future. It was clearly fixed in his mind that he would come to some sort of arrangement with the British, that they would recognize his greatness as an emperor and a man, and treat him accordingly. Whether or not his army was defeated in the field was merely incidental; indeed, he seemed almost eager to see it destroyed by Napier's modern guns.

Yet he proposed to fight. Already in December he had decided to make his stand at Magdala, and with that object he was constructing a road up to the fortress from the Bascillo valley so that his guns and heavy pieces of ordnance would be mounted on the heights. Theodore was not the first or the last man to dream that with the aid of a new and miraculous invention he would put his enemies to flight and save the day at the eleventh hour. His faith was now fixed upon an enormous mortar which his German workmen had made for him. It was an astonishing weapon to have been constructed in these crude surroundings, a solid lump of metal weighing at least seventy tons and shaped like an upended church bell. When filled with pieces of metal and fired by a charge it was expected to produce the loudest and most devastating explosion that had ever been heard in Ethiopia. The mortar was lashed to a heavy wooden gun-carriage, and five hundred men were engaged in dragging it yard by yard over the new road to Magdala.

Every week both the army and the road got a little nearer to the fortress. For the Europeans this was an agonizing time. Hardly a day went by without Rassam receiving a message either from Theodore in the Bascillo valley or from Merewether in the British camp, each of them urging him to keep his spirits up—they were approaching as fast as they could. It was just a question as to whether or not he would receive Theodore's maniac embrace before the friendly British guns arrived. And if the British did arrive and proceed to mount their attack against Magdala, what then? Was Theodore going to let the Europeans go? Or was he going to throw them over the precipice?

Nobody in Ethiopia could answer that question at the moment, least of all the British at Senafé, three hundred and fifty miles away. All that Napier could do was to advance and hope that all would be well. It must have been a wonderful sight to see the column go by, nothing but the wild Ethiopian plain around it, the ragged mountains in the distance, and, just occasionally, on the line of march a tumbledown village where the inhabitants stood like great flocks of birds, chattering, staring and apprehensive.

The cavalry came first, the troopers dressed in crimson caps and green uniforms, and the officers with silver helmets on their heads. Among the infantry that followed on, many of the white men in the Irish regiment wore beards, their cheeks burned a deep brown by the Indian sun, and the native soldiers, the Beloochees, marched along in green tunics with red facings and with large green turbans wound round their fezzes. Others were got up in light blue and silver, or in the regulation scarlet jackets and white turbans, while others again among the European officers sported uniforms of their own design. "One young lordling riding behind Napier," Stanley says, "wore kid gloves and a green veil."

The transport train with the guns and stores came last, and it trailed across the country for seven miles with half the races of

India and the Near East marching in its ranks: Turks, Persians, Egyptians, Arabs, Sikhs, Muslims and Hindus. The sight of the elephants with the heavy guns lashed to their backs and the mahouts sitting on their necks filled the Ethiopian villagers with amazement. Here in Africa the elephant was a wild and savage beast. To see it responding to commands and tamely ambling along almost as if it were a cow or an ox—this was a miracle.

Yet the discipline was strict. "No plundering took place," says the official history of the campaign. Each day reveille was sounded half an hour before dawn, and sometimes they were still on the move at nightfall, but naturally it was not a very rapid progress. They were traveling for the most part along a watershed where the headwaters of many small torrents had cut deep ravines into the plain on their way down to join the Nile, hundreds of miles away in the Sudan. To descend for thousands of feet into one of these ravines, to wait while the sappers threw a bridge across the stream and then to climb back to the plateau on the opposite bank—this could be the work of several days. Many of the mules fell sick at this altitude, and the nights were so cold that every man who could got himself under canvas. Napier's tent, at this early stage of the march, was a lavish affair lined with yellow cotton and carpeted with oriental rugs. Here each night the staff would gather to eat an enormous Victorian dinner, and Napier, if we are to believe Stanley, never failed to charm his guests. He loomed over the gathering, stout, blue-eyed, affable and attentive, a symbol of the days when manners and appearance were still compatible with war, and a general's dinner table was something more than a tray in a cafeteria.

These comfortable effects, however, were drastically reduced as the march went on, and the line of mules and oxen toiling back and forth to the base camp on the coast grew steadily longer. Camp followers and servants were sent back to Zula in hundreds, and the officers' baggage was cut down to 75 lb. From now on even the young lordlings, bereft of their batmen, were "obliged to rely on such assistance as they might obtain from the soldiery." The soldiers on their side were restricted to 25 lb. each, and the rum ration was reduced to one dram a day.

Thus lightened the column struck a faster pace. On February 7 Napier was in Adigrat, and a week later the advance guard reached Antalo, some two hundred miles from the coast and halfway to Magdala. Here a large staging camp was formed and the column was thinned out again. It was like a growing tree, thick at the base where the railway had now reached the mountains and some twenty thousand animals were plying between one depot and the next, and very thin here at the top where only the fighting men and the engineers and their equipment were allowed to pass through. On the way to Antalo came the news that Kassai was approaching with his army, and since Kassai was a valuable ally and this was the first real contact with the Ethiopians Napier halted to receive him with full military honors. The meeting took place on the banks of a small stream where the two commanders, like rival generals conducting a parley in a Shakespearian drama, had each erected a ceremonial tent. Kassai came forward riding on a white mule and with a crimson umbrella held above his head. He was surrounded by about four thousand warriors marching to the sounds of kettledrums and with banners flying. Simultaneously the British approached, Napier riding on an elephant, with an elephant escort and the redcoats drawn up behind. As Kassai drew near it was seen that he was wearing a lion-skin cape and a silk robe embroidered with large flowers, and his hair was bound up in plaits with a ribbon at the back. He was a man of about thirty-five, dark-olive in complexion, and he looked a little harassed and careworn. Fearing treachery, no doubt, he flinched when the redcoats shot off a salute, but the interpreter, Captain Speedy, reassured him, and the two commanders and their staffs entered the British tent. Napier opened the negotiations by presenting Kassai with an Arab charger, a rifle and some pieces of Bohemian glassware. Port wine, taken from the hospital stores, was then drunk, and Napier took care to be the first to raise his glass to his lips to show that it was not poisoned. The Ethiopians were then treated to a display of

British might; the guns were deployed, the infantry skirmished and formed square, and the cavalry in full ceremonial uniform dashed back and forth before the tent.

After this Kassai warmly assured the British that he would do everything in his power to assist them by providing food and fodder on the line of march, and Napier was now invited to cross with his staff to the Ethiopian tent. Here they were waited upon by Ethiopian girls. Bread and curry were served together with huge bullock horns filled with tej that were instantly replenished when they were emptied. While they ate and drank musicians with long pipes appeared and a minstrel singer, improvising as he went along, welcomed the British to Ethiopia. Napier was then draped with a lion-skin cape, and with a sword, a shield and a spear in his hands was mounted on a grey mule. Thus bedecked he rode back to the British lines under the curious eyes of his own soldiers.

The honors in this game had not altogether gone to the British. In the Ethiopian camp they had been very much struck by Kassai's warriors, their toughness and air of independence, and it was something of a surprise to find that almost every man was equipped with a serviceable rifle. Theodore presumably possessed just such guerrilla fighters as these, and Magdala, with its thousand-foot precipices, still lay two hundred miles away with many dangerous passes in between. Somewhat more cautiously the army pushed on again, and on March 17 Napier and his headquarters, following in the wake of the advance guard, reached Lake Ashangi, one hundred miles from Magdala. They were now in a region of 9,000-foot passes, and the tracks up the cliffs were so steep and narrow that if one animal stopped all stopped. Sometimes when the guns were being hauled up and down ravines the whole column was wedged for an hour or more in an immovable traffic block. Tremendous thunderstorms swept the mountains almost every day, and the men were forced to march in sopping clothing with temperatures down to zero.

A further lightening of the baggage was now ordered and this meant that many of the soldiers were obliged to sleep out in the open at night and make do with half the normal rations. Constant rumors of the approach of the enemy passed along the column, but still no shot had been fired, and the sentries posted around the camps at night had nothing more dangerous to contend with than prowling hyenas and an occasional lion roaring over a kill in the darkness. On March 28 the advance guard reached the Takkazé River, forty miles in a direct line from Magdala. The two armies, Theodore in the south on the Bascillo and Napier here in the north on the Takkazé, were now rapidly converging on one another, and the tension among the prisoners in Magdala had become extreme.

It was now more than four years since Cameron and his staff had been imprisoned, and all of them had been in chains for nearly two years, since the middle of 1866. During that long time they had learned to live from day to day with a certain fatalism, but this new element of tantalizing hope was difficult to bear. Every messenger from the emperor's camp was closely questioned about Theodore's changing moods, every morning they went to the ramparts hoping to see some sign of the approach of the British. Theodore in his letters to the prisoners continued to be remarkably benign, and on March 5 Rassam was overwhelmed to hear that his fetters were to be removed. "Some of the chiefs," Rassam says, "assisted in striking off my fetters, whilst others placed their fingers between the iron and the flesh to prevent my ankles from being hurt."

Two days later Flad arrived with the news that the road up to Magdala was almost complete, and it was plain that Theodore intended to get up to the Magdala heights before the British appeared. During the next few days more of the royal treasure was brought into Magdala, and from the ramparts the prisoners could see the advance guard of the Ethiopian army making camp on the plain of Salamgie, directly below the entrance gate. On March 27 Theodore himself arrived. Surprisingly, he made no attempt to see Rassam or the prisoners; he proceeded directly to the church to worship, and afterwards set himself up on his throne outside his palace. Here he sat for several hours receiving the trembling Magdala chiefs and accusing them of high treason in his absence. In the evening, having assured Rassam by letter that he would send for him shortly, he returned to his camp below the mountain, apparently in a black mood. That night fresh guards were placed on the European prisoners, and they were markedly and ominously hostile. Rassam, who was now in daily communication with the British camp, burnt all the letters he received. There is something elusive about Rassam. Helpless though they all were in Magdala, he seems at times a little too soft, too compliant, too yielding for his own good. Might not a less subtle and more downright man have made a stronger impression on Theodore and have brought him to his senses long before this? Theodore clearly saw in Rassam another courtier, a most interesting and valuable one, and it was very flattering to his ego to have in his power this foreign envoy always smiling and humbly submitting, no matter how badly he was treated.

This perhaps is putting Rassam's case in too harsh a light, but still one would have liked a word from Consul Cameron, or from one of the other Europeans, on these matters. Did they all agree with the way Rassam was handling things? Or was it simply that, in their misery and uncertainty, they were prepared to accept any leadership? And since Rassam's policy was patience and submissiveness were they swept along with it from day to day? It is only fair to add that Rassam thought throughout that he was acting for the best; he behaved towards Theodore as his instincts and his nature impelled him to do, and he was not without courage.

Now, at all events, he got into his blue uniform as soon as Theodore reappeared in Magdala, and presently he was summoned by an escort. He was met by an extraordinary sight when he emerged from the prisoners' compound. About two thousand square yards of the open ground had been covered with oriental rugs, and the emperor's ceremonial tent was set up at one end with a great gathering of chiefs around it. Theodore himself was closeted in the tent with his German artisans, but he came forward eagerly to shake hands with Rassam, saying, "Today we must all be English." It was nearly two years since they had met, and Rassam was astonished at his appearance. His hair had gone grey and he looked ten years older. Noticing Rassam's surprise, Theodore said, "Look at me, and see how grey I have become since we parted . . . One day you may see me dead and while you stand by my corpse it may be that you will curse me. You may say then, 'This wicked man ought not to be buried; let his remains rot above ground,' but I trust in your generosity." Rassam begged that he would not mention such a calamity.

For the rest, Rassam goes on, Theodore's "politeness was extreme, and he was all smiles, except when alluding to Consul Cameron. . . ." He toasted Rassam's health in tej, he roared with laughter at Rassam's jokes, and he instantly agreed that Prideaux and Blanc at least should be released from their fetters. On the subject of the approaching British army he was remarkably complacent: they were aware that he was the descendant of Solomon, King of Kings, and all would be well. "I hope, Mr. Rassam," he added, "that when your people arrive they will not despise me because I am black; God has given us all the same faculties and heart." With this the interview closed and Theodore descended again to his camp at Salamgie.

Four days later a second meeting took place. Rassam, Blanc and Prideaux were invited to witness the arrival of the great mortar, and on going down the mountain they found Theodore sitting on the edge of a precipice superintending the operations. The mortar was being hauled up a steep patch of the new road at an angle of forty-five degrees, and for a time it looked as though it would break away from its traces and go thundering down the valley. When it reached level ground at last Theodore turned to Rassam and questioned him about the British army—how powerful were their guns, how far could they shoot, how did the soldiers maneuver? Rassam said he knew nothing of military matters and Theodore went on: "How can I show these ragged soldiers of mine to your well-dressed troops . . . ? Were I as powerful as I once was, I should certainly have gone down to the coast to meet your people on landing; or I would have sent and asked them what they wanted in my country. As it is,

I have lost all Abyssinia but this rock." The mortar, he added, had been made not to be used against the British but his own countrymen. Then again he returned to his grievances against Cameron and the other prisoners, and it was some time before Rassam could bring him round to a better mood. In the end he agreed that Cameron and all the others who were still in chains should be released, and on returning to the compound in the afternoon Rassam found that the order had already been carried out.

Throughout this meeting Theodore had been rather muted, even a little pathetic, and the prisoners' hopes were further raised that night when a messenger arrived from Merewether saying that the army was now advancing beyond the Takkazé.

During the next six days the prisoners heard very little from Theodore. It was said that he had gone off on a plundering expedition in the Bascillo valley and that, on his return to his camp, he did nothing each day but ascend to the neighboring height of Selassie with his telescope to scan the horizon for the British troops.

Napier was now making excellent headway. On April 5 they reached Theodore's new road on the Chetta River, and at once they began the descent into the Bascillo valley, which was some three thousand nine hundred feet below the general level of the country. Magdala, only ten miles away, was now clearly visible, and Napier, on going ahead to reconnoiter, was not reassured. "Altogether, without taking into account Magdala itself," he wrote later in his dispatches, "the formidable character of its outworks exceeded anything which we could possibly have anticipated. . . ." Three flat-topped peaks, each about nine thousand feet in height, rose before them: Fahla on the right, Selassie (whence Theodore was now gazing down on them) on the left, and finally Magdala itself. Whether or not Theodore gave battle either on the Aroge plateau before Fahla, or on the Salamgie plain, Magdala itself would have to be taken by assault. While the main gate was forced by a frontal attack an attempt would have to be made to climb the thousand-foot cliffs of the fortress with the aid of scaling ladders—one of the most dangerous operations imaginable. That night Napier completed his plans.

About two thousand men were to go into the attack, each carrying in addition to his rifle and ammunition four pounds of rations and a water bottle which was to be filled in the Bascillo River at the time of the crossing. Sappers and infantry were to lead the way with the guns coming up behind, and the cavalry was to be held in reserve. To prevent Theodore from beating a retreat at the last moment, the Galla tribesmen were to be asked to surround the fortress while the battle was going on—a duty which they were very willing to undertake since Theodore within the past week had utterly ravaged the country around Magdala, and their hatred of him had risen to a frenzy.

Despite his constant communication with Rassam, Napier had difficulty in making any precise estimate of the enemy's strength, but he judged it to be around seven thousand fighting men, most of them equipped with rifles and supported by the mortar and several batteries of guns. If they chose to make a strong stand at Magdala they could certainly inflict heavy casualties and withstand a siege of weeks or even months. For the moment, however, it appeared that Theodore was deploying on the Salamgie plain; from April 5 onwards the British could clearly see his tents and the smoke of his army's cooking fires. Napier sent off a native messenger with his final ultimatum: "By the command of the Queen of England I am approaching Magdala with my army, in order to recover from your hands Envoy Rassam, Dr. Blanc, Lieutenant Prideaux, and the other Europeans now in your Majesty's power. I request your Majesty to send them to my camp as soon as it is sufficiently near to admit of their coming in safety."

The final forced marches were particularly severe. Rain and hailstorms drenched the men by night, and by day the clear mountain sun was unbearably hot. The elephants were in great distress. They slipped and fell on the wet ground, and for a time some of them refused to go on. When the baggage train fell further and further behind on the narrow tracks many of the men went for thirty-six hours or more without food—and this at the end of an exhausting four-hundred-mile march from the coast. But it was a stimulating thing to see the enemy at last, after three long months in Ethiopia, and the official dispatches are probably not exaggerating when they say that the men, Indians and British alike, went forward with enthusiasm. By the night of April 9 the assault force was congregated on the Bascillo, and on the following morning, Good Friday, they crossed the stream barefooted, stooping to fill their water bottles on the way. Then, in dead silence, they began climbing the escarpment on the opposite side. They had about five miles to go to reach their first objective, the Aroge plateau.

Theodore meanwhile had posted his mortar and seven guns on the heights of Fahla, while he himself, with the bulk of his men, still remained encamped about a mile and a half further back on the Salamgie plain. At dawn on April 8 Rassam received a message to say that he and all the prisoners, European as well as native, were to descend at once to this camp. They found Theodore dressed in white pantaloons and a robe of Lyons silk worked with gold. "He looked," says Rassam, "more like a harlequin than a sovereign in this novel motley suit"; but his manner was anything but gay. Rassam found an opportunity of asking him why he did not enter into negotiations with Napier. "What is the use of it?" Theodore answered. "The die is cast. Things must take their course." He went off then to Selassie with his telescope, and when he returned in the afternoon he told the British prisoners that he had seen a line of elephants laden with baggage coming up the Bascillo valley. He seemed to be in a detached and exalted mood. Nearly six hundred native prisoners had been brought down from Magdala with the Europeans, and in the course of the day most of the women and children, one hundred and eighty-six in all, were released, together with thirty-seven chiefs.

The Europeans spent the night in their pavilion, and on the following morning they heard that Theodore had declared a general amnesty. It was a long business, however, getting the fetters opened; by four in the afternoon only ninety-five men had been released, and some of the other prisoners, mostly

Gallas, began to complain of the delay. As though he had been waiting for something of this sort to occur, Theodore suddenly went berserk. He rushed out of his tent, sword in hand, and ran with his bodyguard to the huts where the native prisoners were quartered, close to the edge of a precipice. The Europeans were ordered to stay in their tent and did not see the massacre that followed, but they heard the shots being fired and the shouts and screams of the victims. For two hours the prisoners were dragged before Theodore one after another. Hardly any of them had committed any crime more serious than having laughed in Theodore's presence when he was in a black humor or perhaps having failed to hand him a gun or a sword at the right moment. For this they had remained for months, even years, in chains and were now assassinated. He listened, insane with rage, as each wretch was led up to him and the charge was read out, and the verdict was almost always the same: "Take him away." The man was then pitched over the precipice, and those that survived the fall were shot dead by riflemen posted in the ravine below. The killing went on until nightfall before he had had enough, and by that time one hundred and ninety-seven bodies lay mangled on the rocks below.

Throughout that night the camp lay still, apprehensive and silent. Theodore slept very little. His servants said later that he passed most of the night drinking and praying. Over and over again he fell on his knees pleading for forgiveness for the massacre he had just committed. In the morning of April 10 the European prisoners were told that Theodore had changed his mind about them: they were to return at once to Magdala, and they were advised to move off without delay since he was still in a savage humor. Rassam, however, made one more effort to get him to open negotiations with Napier. Theodore replied to his letter: "Do you want me to write to that man? No, I will do nothing of the kind since he has been sent here by a woman."

As the Europeans were leaving the camp Napier's messenger arrived and the ultimatum was handed to Rassam. He at once sent a further note to Theodore asking for permission to bring the messenger before him. Theodore replied by letter, refusing to see either the ultimatum or the messenger. "If you yourself communicate with the British," he added, "my friendship with you will cease and the blood of your messenger will be on your head. Beware."

On returning to their compound in Magdala the Europeans found the place deserted; many of the civilians had decamped in the night, and barely fifty fighting men were left to defend the fortress. The day had broken grey and sultry, and huge thunderclouds were building up over the mountains.

CHAPTER TWELVE

THE DEATH OF THEODORE

THERE is a strong atmosphere of fantasy about the Battle of Magdala, and it is not entirely confined to the part played by the Emperor Theodore. In a sense, of course, all battles are fantastic, since they are a deliberate courting of death, but here most of the normal conditions of war seem to be lacking, the pattern is wrong, far too much is being done for too small an object.

In Ethiopia the British sought no gain of any kind, and they had no quarrel with the Ethiopian people. Once the prisoners had been released they were determined to go away and leave the country to its own dark devices. In other words, the whole vast expensive operation was nothing more nor less than a matter of racial pride; Theodore had affronted a great power and now he was to be punished.

And so to settle an issue of pride, one man's pride against a nation's, we have now the extraordinary spectacle of two armies advancing against one another high up in this remote aerie in the Ethiopian mountains. These armies are ignorant beyond dreams; they know nothing of one another's language, politics or way of life. They have no real hatred of one another, and no real interest in the quarrel. Yet someone orders them to fight and off they go, Christians and Muhammadans, blacks and whites, Sikhs, Hindus and Ethiopian tribesmen, believing implicitly that the action to which they are committed—the killing of one another—is absolutely inevitable and right.

Soon after the European prisoners had left his camp on Good Friday morning Theodore received word that the British were approaching the Aroge plateau in two columns, one of them using the new road and the other climbing up directly from the Bascillo valley. He at once went off with the German engineers to the heights of Fahla to take command of the artillery, while the remainder of his force, about seven thousand men, placed themselves in readiness on the lower slopes of the mountain. The command of the army was given to a chieftain named Gabry who had been born in Theodore's province and who had followed him loyally through all his campaigns.

There seems to have been no plan of battle, merely a general understanding that as soon as the British came in sight the artillery would open fire and the tribesmen would charge. Loot was to be their reward.

Meanwhile the British were finding the ascent from the Bascillo much tougher than they had expected. Despite the gathering thunderstorm the heat was intense, and many of the men, after several hours of climbing upward, fell out exhausted. Thus it was not until four o'clock in the afternoon that the two columns began to debouch onto the Aroge plateau, and at that moment a puff of white smoke curled upwards from the summit of Fahla. It was followed by a heavy detonation that echoed and re-echoed round the cliffs, and a shell, whirring over the heads of Napier and his staff, buried itself in the ground behind. Then all the lower slopes of Fahla became filled with rushing men heading for the plateau, the chiefs, about five hundred of them, dressed in scarlet and riding horses, and the spearsmen running in between. It was estimated later that there were some five thousand warriors in the charge, all of them singing their war songs as they came on.

Napier had just sufficient time to deploy. He ordered his infantry to drop their packs on the ground and to advance in line, while his battery of rockets opened up over their heads at the approaching enemy. There was a decided wavering in the charge as the rockets exploded, but the Ethiopians still came on. The storm had now burst, and the noise of thunder was added to the cracking of the cannon and the shouts and cheers of both armies as they ran forward for the clash. At most places the Ethiopians were stopped in their tracks by rifle fire when they were still one hundred yards or more from the British, but some of them broke through and for a few moments tackled the British swordsmen with their spears. In general, however, it was an indiscriminate killing. The great mortar on Fahla burst at its first discharge and soon after this the rest of the Ethiopian guns stopped altogether. Their wild and erratic shooting had accomplished nothing. And now, as more and more British entered the battle and got their guns into position, a general massacre began in the rain. It was thought that the chief Gabry was Theodore himself, since he was more gorgeously attired than the other horsemen, and he was soon cut down. From this time onwards it was simply a question of how many Ethiopians could be killed before the daylight failed. Even when all hope had gone they would not give up. They rallied again and again, and came on into the rifle fire, each charge getting a little feebler than the last, and it was not until seven o'clock, after three hours of continuous fighting, that the last Ethiopian was driven off the plateau. Fearing that his men would get lost in the darkness Napier broke off the pursuit, and the army was ordered to bivouac where it was for the night while further reinforcements came up from the Bascillo. In the dusk some 700 Ethiopian dead were counted on the battlefield and their wounded were estimated at 1,200. The British losses were twenty wounded, of whom two died later on.

For a few hours lights kept flickering on the slopes of Fahla, but Theodore made no attempt to renew the attack, and all through that night the wounded could be heard crying on the battlefield. A few of these men were got into the British hospital and the remainder were either carried off by their comrades in the darkness or managed to crawl away of their own accord.

We have a fairly full account of Theodore's movements through these hours. He seems to have made some attempt to restrain his men from charging at first, but gave in when he found that they were determined and then took up his position on Fahla, saying that he would cover them with his artillery.

He ordered the German workmen to measure out the charges for the mortar and the guns, but the actual firing was carried out by his own men. Quite early in the action the British rockets found the range on Fahla and Theodore was nearly killed by one of them. From then onwards he covered himself with his shield and watched the battle in silence, constantly sending messengers down the mountain to ask Gabry and the other chiefs for news. But the messengers could bring back no news except that all the chiefs were dead. Soon after nightfall he retired to his camp at Salamgie.

The prisoners, meanwhile, cooped up in Magdala, had spent an agitated day. They heard the firing on the Aroge plateau but it was too far off to make out what was happening, and no news of any kind arrived. Soon after dark Rassam went to bed, but he was woken at 10:30 p.m. by Flad and one of the Germans bearing a message from Theodore. It ran as follows: "How have you passed the day? Thank God, I am well. I, being a King, could not allow people to come and fight me without attacking them first. I have done so and my troops have been beaten. I thought your people were women but I find they are men. They fought very bravely. Seeing that I am not able to withstand them, I must ask you to reconcile me to them."

Rassam at once wrote a reply saying that Theodore should send off a deputation to Napier at dawn the following morning, and he suggested that both Flad and Prideaux should be members of the party. Theodore's son-in-law, Dejach Alami, was to accompany them.

At dawn on April 11 the British outposts caught sight of a little group approaching, carrying a white flag, and there was a great shout of excitement when it was seen that there was a British uniform (Prideaux's) among them. With cheering soldiers pressing round them the party was quickly passed through to Napier's tent on the further side of the Aroge plateau. They gave the General a verbal message from Theodore saying that he wanted "a reconciliation," and Napier drafted the following reply:

"Your Majesty has fought like a brave man, and has been overcome by the superior power of the British Army. It is my desire that no more blood may be shed. If, therefore, your Majesty will submit to the Queen of England, and bring all the Europeans now in your Majesty's hands, and deliver them safely, this day, in the British Camp, I guarantee honorable treatment for yourself, and all the members of your Majesty's family."

This message was buttressed by a threat: the son-in-law, Dejach Alami, was shown the elephants and the heavy guns which had now been brought up, and was told that the weapons which the British had used on the previous day were nothing but playthings to those that would now be employed unless Theodore surrendered. If he tried to escape he would be pursued to the ends of Ethiopia. Dejach Alami was also informed that reprisals would be taken upon him and the other chieftains if they failed to restrain Theodore from further brutalities.

Somewhat shaken by this, Dejach Alami pleaded for a twenty-four hours' delay, which was granted, and Flad and Prideaux, with some misgivings no doubt, returned with him to the emperor's camp. Theodore questioned them very closely about the exact meaning of Napier's letter. What did he mean by honorable treatment? Did they intend to treat him as a prisoner or were they going to assist him in recovering his country from the rebels? And did the British really intend to look after his family?—it was very numerous. He seemed to be in a repressed and dangerous mood again.

Moreover, the reply that Theodore now sent back to Napier was hardly a good augury. He did not mention the prisoners. He did not refer to his own surrender. Instead he declaimed against his own people for their cowardice in battle, their hatred towards him, their irreligion. But then, as though he himself had already passed from the scene, he appealed to Napier, in Biblical language, to look after them:

"In my city there are multitudes whom I have fed: maidens protected and maidens unprotected; women whom yesterday made widows; and aged parents who have no children. God has given you the power. See that you forsake not these people. It is a heathen land....

"I had intended, if God had so decreed, to conquer the whole world; and it was my desire to die if my purpose could not be fulfilled. Since the day of my birth till now no man has dared to lay hand on me. Whenever my soldiers began to waver in battle, it was for me to arise and rally them. Last night the darkness prevented me from doing so. A warrior who has dandled strong men in his arms like infants will never suffer himself to be dandled in the arms of others."

This letter, together with the letter Theodore had already received from Napier, was handed to Prideaux and Flad and they were told to return alone to the British camp.

Soon after they had gone Theodore called a council of war, and at this meeting a strong group of his chiefs pressed for the murder of the European prisoners and a renewal of hostilities. Theodore disapproved, saying that if the prisoners were murdered Napier was bound to take reprisals; they must be released. Towards four in the afternoon a group of chiefs were sent up to Magdala with orders to bring Rassam and the other Europeans down to the camp.

Throughout these discussions Theodore had seemed relatively calm, but now suddenly, while awaiting the arrival of the prisoners, he flew into a violent spasm of rage. He picked up his double-barrelled pistol, thrust it into his mouth and pulled the trigger. Apparently he had cocked the wrong barrel, for there was no explosion, and one of his men rushed at him and tore the weapon away. In the scuffle the bullet went off and grazing Theodore's ear expended itself harmlessly in the air. Theodore then covered his head with a cloth and lay down on the ground.

Up to this point no one dreamed that Theodore would ever let the prisoners go, and it was now regarded as almost certain that, in his present delirium, he would have them shot when they entered the camp. The prisoners felt this too, and they came down the steep track from Magdala in silence and with the utmost dread. As they were approaching the camp they were told that the emperor had left his tent and was now awaiting them on the road that led down to the British lines. He wanted to see Rassam alone. Leaving the others behind in a group on the roadside, Rassam went forward and found Theodore standing among about twenty of his bodyguard and the German engineers. He was at once beckoned forward, and Theodore asked him how he had passed the day. Then, looking up towards the sun, Theodore said: "Do you not think it is late for you to go this afternoon to your camp? Would you rather go at once or spend the night with me, and in the morning I will send you straight to your people?"

Rassam answered that he would do whatever Theodore pleased, and Theodore answered, "Good; you had better go now. But sit down for a moment and let me have a few words with you before you leave." They sat together on the ground, and Theodore went on, "You know, Mr. Rassam, you and I have always been on good terms. God knows your heart, but as far as I am concerned I have always had a sincere regard for you. It is true that I have behaved badly towards you, but that was because of the behavior of bad men. However, the past cannot be helped now, and I can only say, God's will be done. I want you to bear this in mind—that unless you befriend me I shall either kill myself or become a monk. Now, good-bye; it's getting late; try and come to see me tomorrow if you can."

"I then thanked him for his kindness," Rassam writes, "and said, 'I will come and see your Majesty if possible.' He asked again, 'Will you come tomorrow?' I replied that it all depended on the orders of the Commander in Chief. He then rose, shook hands with me, wept and said, 'Farewell; be quick, it is getting late.' "

This presented an agonizing difficulty. The rest of the prisoners, including Cameron, whom Theodore hated, were still in a group further up the road. If Rassam walked on alone there was still no guarantee that Theodore might not suddenly order them to be shot down as they went past him. His bodyguard were standing ready with their rifles. Rassam said, "I thank your Majesty, but my companions are behind."

"His only answer," Rassam continues, "was—and these words

were the last I heard from his lips—'You had better go.' I was now anxious about my fellow-captives, and after walking on a few paces I stopped. The King was still standing on a rock, surrounded by his musketeers, and holding a double-barrelled rifle in his hands. When he saw me stop and look round, he motioned me with his hand to go on. My fears then began to increase; still, I apprehended that if I said anything we should all be shot down, so I proceeded a few steps farther and stood still, when, to my intense joy, I saw my fellow-captives coming down the hill towards me."

On their way into the British camp they met Flad and Prideaux who were returning to Theodore with a message from Napier saying that he could offer no other terms. Since most of the prisoners were now released there was no point in Flad and Prideaux again putting themselves into Theodore's hands that night, and they turned back with the others. The whole party entered the British lines soon after dusk and was received with some emotion in Napier's tent.

The next evening, Sunday, April 12, all the remaining Europeans were safely brought down to the British. Through the course of the day Theodore sent down one thousand cows and five hundred sheep—all he possessed—to the British camp, and for a time he seems to have been under the impression that they had been accepted. Napier, however, had been informed that, by Ethiopian custom, if he accepted the gift he was morally bound to conclude peace, and the herds were consequently turned back by the pickets.

When on the Sunday evening Theodore heard this news, he exclaimed, "These people, having got what they want, now seek to kill me," and in a fury rushed up the path to Magdala calling on his chiefs and soldiers to follow him. He seems to have had some confused idea of escaping on foot by way of a steep path that led down from the ramparts on the eastern side of the fortress, and he planned, he said, to make his way back to Lake Tana and the Blue Nile. About two thousand men followed him at first, but it was a hopeless venture; the Gallas were lying in ambush all round the mountain hoping that just such an attempt would be made, and when his followers began to turn back Theodore himself returned to Magdala. Bitter arguments appear to have continued there through most of the night, Theodore accusing his chiefs of cowardice, and the chiefs replying that he must either surrender or fight; they refused to follow him into retreat since it meant leaving their families and possessions behind. In the end the chiefs agreed among themselves that surrender was the only course, and they decided that if Theodore attempted to carry out any further executions they would seize him and put him in chains. During the night thousands of warriors with their families began to decamp to the British lines.

The end was now coming very close. Theodore got up at dawn on Monday, April 13, determined that he himself at least would not surrender. He descended the mountain once more to Salamgie with some forty or fifty men who still remained loyal to him, and together they tried to move a battery of heavy guns up the precipitous path to the gate of the fortress. It was an absurd project, and they were interrupted in the midst of it by the appearance of a party of British cavalry. This was too much for Theodore's overburdened mind. He jumped on his horse and began to ride furiously back and forth across the plain, shouting out boasts of his own prowess, firing his rifle in the air, and challenging the British to single combat. When no notice was taken of him he was induced at last by some of his men to retire up the path to Magdala. Here, with a little handful to help him, he set to work piling up huge stones against the entrance gate. They were still engaged on this work at one in the afternoon when the first British shells began to fall.

Napier had decided to give Theodore a little further time to surrender—a little more rope with which to hang himself—but on hearing during the night a rumor that he had escaped he had decided on immediate action. Messages were sent to the Galla tribesmen offering a reward of fifty thousand dollars for the capture of the emperor, dead or alive, and in the British camp some three thousand men with artillery support were ordered into the assault. By 8:30 a.m. on April 13 they had covered all the approaches to the Magdala gate, and it was a little after this that the squadron of cavalry had surprised Theodore on the Salamgie plain. Refugees were now streaming down towards the British lines on every side, and the infantry were obliged to pass through them as they advanced in skirmishing order to the foot of the Magdala cliffs. The first salvoes of rockets were directed on the gate, a pagoda-like affair with a roof and two heavy wooden doors, and the assaulting parties immediately went forward with scaling ladders, some of them using the path, while others scrambled directly up the cliffs towards the ramparts. It was a long climb; rain was falling again, and the noise of thunder combined with the crashing of shells above their heads. Towards 4 p.m. the advance guard reached the gate and here they came under rifle fire while they hacked away at the doors with crowbars. It was not a very heavy fire—only a handful of the enemy were shooting at them from above—but nine of the British went down before they forced their way through. Simultaneously the party that had scaled the ramparts came running in behind the gate from the flank. The little group of defenders now retreated to a second, smaller, gate about seventy yards further up, losing most of their number on the way. This second gate was open, and the British rushed through it on to the Magdala plateau, only to discover that all resistance had collapsed. From every direction Ethiopians came forward to surrender, and presently the watchers on the plain below saw the Union Jack go up on the ramparts. The total British casualties were just fifteen wounded.

On the path leading up to the palace from the second gate a dead man was found lying alone on the ground, and no one took much notice of him at first. Yet this was the Emperor Theodore. He had led the resistance at the gate and had gone on firing until it had been broken down. Retreating then through the second gate, he had told his last surviving followers to escape, and had taken his pistol in his hand—one of those same pistols that Plowden had given him so long ago as a gift from Queen Victoria. He had put the muzzle in his mouth, and this time he had not misfired. Rassam, following in the wake of the assault troops, was called to identify the body. Its clothing was already much torn and pulled about by souvenir hunters, and he remembered the voice saying, "One day you may see me dead and while you stand by my corpse it may be that you will curse me. You may say 'This wicked man ought not to be buried; let his remains rot above ground,' but I trust in your generosity." Rassam had the body taken up and carried to his old quarters in the European compound, where it was covered by a shroud and laid out on a bed.

On the following day Theodore was buried in Magdala church by Coptic priests, and it was, Rassam says, "an affecting sight to witness the reverence with which the dignitaries of the Church performed these last offices for their departed Sovereign; even in death Theodore had not wholly lost the affection of at least some of his subjects."

In Magdala meanwhile there was utter confusion. A few of the Ethiopian soldiers had tried to escape by way of the footpath on the eastern side, but they had been immediately confronted by Galla tribesmen who, according to one eyewitness, had cried out to them, "Come, beloved, come"—at which they had turned back and had joined in the general surrender.

The looting began about 4:30 p.m. with the breaking open of the treasury and the royal palace, and there were some very spectacular things to be had since Theodore had collected here all the remaining ancient treasure of the Ethiopian kings: gold chalices, miters and crowns; goblets, ornaments studded with precious stones, gifts from foreign monarchs, cases of champagne and other wines, silk tents, carpets, furs, lion-skin capes, ornamented saddles, state umbrellas, swords, embroidered robes, parchments and official papers galore. All these, Stanley says, were tossed about and quarreled over by soldiers and civilians, and some of the worst of the looters, he asserts, were the European prisoners who had come back to Magdala after the assault.

The arrival of Napier quieted the worst of these disturbances. A brass band preceded him, and he marched with his staff and flagbearers through the gate to the strains of "Here the Conquering Hero Comes." One of his first acts was to release about ninety Ethiopians who were still manacled in the prison, and to make arrangements for the civilian population. Apart from the sixty Ethiopians who had been killed and the 120 who had been wounded in the fighting, about 4,000 people had been found in the fortress and it was clear they could not stay where they were. There was an extreme shortage of water on the plateau, and under cover of the drunkenness and looting many private scores were being paid off.

A general evacuation of the fortress was therefore ordered, and in batches the Ethiopian families were escorted down the hill to the British camp where they were safe from the Gallas. Among the first to go were Theodore's family: his beautiful young wife, Teru-Wark, and her child Alamayo: Teru-Wark said that it had been Theodore's wish that his son should go to England, and that she would willingly follow him there. She was, however, sad, silent, and dejected as Rassam took her down the mountain—a thing that struck him as strange since she had never been loved by Theodore, even though it was said that he had become reconciled to her a few days before he died.

Theodore's empire had now collapsed entirely, and all northern and central Ethiopia were divided into belligerent tribal camps, all hating one another, all ready for civil war once the British had departed.

Napier does not appear to have bothered himself too much with the problem; his orders were to rescue the prisoners and then get out of the country as quickly as possible. He had no intention whatever of paying any attention to Theodore's appeal: "See that you forsake not these people." In the end he simply dodged the issue: the Queen of the Gallas was installed as ruler of Magdala and the surrounding country, and the larger question of Theodore's successor was left hanging in the air. One can only observe that the manner by which the British left Ethiopia did not become them so well as their manner of entering it.

The last act at Magdala was hardly more than a cock-crow

of triumph and revenge. By April 16 all the civilians had been evacuated from the fortress, and fifteen of the elephants brought down the loot to the plain below. On the following day engineers blew the breeches of Theodore's guns, and all the larger buildings except the church were mined. At 4 p.m. the great explosion went up. Fire spread rapidly from hut to hut, with shells and cartridges erupting in the flames, and for many miles around soldiers and tribesmen stood in awe as a vast pall of smoke went up. The fires were still burning with a fierce red glow when darkness fell, and in the morning all that was left of the fortress of Magdala was ash.

By this time the homeward march had already begun, but on April 18 there was a pause on the far side of the Bascillo when Napier made a public declaration of thanks to his soldiers and the loot was auctioned. Holmes of the British Museum was one of the biggest bidders—some 900 volumes of manuscripts had been saved—and at the end of the sale a total of $14,000 was collected. This was distributed to the soldiers according to rank.

All military retreats, whether from victory or defeat, have an air of anticlimax, and this one was no exception; it was simply more colorful than most. The men were very tired, and some of the elephants lay down miserably on the ground, refusing to get up and go on any more. They were shot. It was still an imposing procession, with the bands playing and the flags leading the way, but the army soon learned that they had earned no gratitude in Ethiopia; they were treated as simply another warlike tribe on the move, and now that they were going away like weak and defeated men they were an obvious target for attack.

Tribesmen perched themselves on the heights above the passes and fired down on the weaker parts of the column, hoping for plunder. From time to time forays had to be sent out against them, and food and fodder that was offered for sale on the outward journey now had to be seized by force. Heavy rain followed the army all the way, and when the baggage animals began to die en masse great quantities of stores were either abandoned or blown up.

By the middle of May Napier and his staff were halfway

down to the coast at Antalo, and here Queen Teru-Wark collapsed. She had grown steadily weaker since leaving Magdala, and although Rassam and Napier's doctor plied her with port wine and arrowroot she soon refused to eat.

At the height of a night storm at Antalo servants came running to Rassam with the news that she was dead. He had her buried by the local Coptic priests, and the little boy Alamayo continued on with the British under the care of a nurse.[1]

The column was now rolling itself up like an enormous carpet, and although a hundred vessels were already taking off the forward units from Zula there was great need for haste. The rains grew heavier every day, and the dry bed of the Kumayli River was soon submerged by a racing torrent. It carried away seven men and many animals in a cloudburst near the Suru Pass, and for some days the tail of the column was held up.

By June 2, however, they were all through and Napier and his staff reached the coast. Every movable object at Zula was now taken up and loaded onto the ships: the telegraph, the railway lines, the salt-water condensers, the thirty-nine surviving elephants. Except for the wharves and a few locomotives hardly anything remained to show that the British had ever been in Ethiopia. On June 10 Napier embarked on the *Feroze* and sailed direct for Suez and England. Not unnaturally a tumultuous welcome was awaiting him: the thanks of Parliament, a gracious reception by the Queen, a step up in the service and a peerage.

Lord Napier of Magdala was the hero of the day. Nor were his men forgotten. Among the many favors bestowed among them there was a grant of $14,000 for Rassam and $5,600 apiece for Blanc and Prideaux.

It had been a great thing to take part in the Magdala campaign and now that it was all over it could be forgotten. Ethiopia, with her defenses breached, her lesson learned and her people abandoned to their natural anarchy, slipped quietly out of the news.

[1] He was taken to England on Napier's ship and was subsequently sent to school at Rugby, but he died when he was nineteen and was buried at St. George's Chapel, Windsor.

EPILOGUE

EVEN by the 1950s very little was known about the Blue Nile gorge. The planners and the road builders avoided it where they could, and the Ethiopians, even with the aid of DDT to fight malaria, had no desire to go down into those depths which had always had a name for superstition and evil. But by the 1960s the westernization of Ethiopia had reached a point where it had become necessary to investigate the resources of the river. An American survey team was brought in, and now for the first time the gorge was studied in detail; engineers in helicopters were able to fly down to the most hidden corners.

The writer was fortunate in being able to spend a day on one of these excursions, and it was a revelation of a kind, rather like that moment when one first put on a diving mask and explored the bottom of the sea. We took off early one morning from Addis Ababa and flew directly to the river, one hundred miles away. The helicopter, skimming along only ten yards above the ground, was a madly strange thing in these regions, and the villagers uncovered their heads and bowed to us as we went by. All around them the undulating plateau spread away, dotted with eucalyptus groves, and a hundred little streams and waterfalls rushed down to the great curving valley of the river nearly a mile below. Coming up to the edge of this valley one sank, as in an elevator, into the gorge itself, down and down, past scattered forests and cliffs of glaring black rock and gravel.

As we descended the walls of the gorge came steadily closer and the sky above contracted into a narrow arch of light. Finally we hovered over the river itself, and it was full of movement: it coursed along only one hundred feet across at the narrower places, greenish-grey in color, and at every bend in its winding course it broke into eddies and whirlpools that would have been very difficult to negotiate in a boat. This was in January, when the river is low, but by the end of the wet season in July it would be another thirty feet higher and the current twice as fast. Except where a tributary came in and stained the clear water with a murky grey the banks presented an unbroken cliff-face not too steep for a man to clamber along perhaps, but impossible for a mule. For a while we shot upstream, and it was an exhilarating thing to sit there in our absurd transparent box, seeing everything with an eagle's eye, and being too absorbed to be afraid. At first no human beings anywhere appeared, but there was a good deal of wild game on the sandbanks and occasional flat ledges of ground: storks and other wading birds among the reeds, waterhogs, blacker even than this black sand, kneeling to drink, small herds of antelopes, a hippopotamus or two mooning in the deeper pools and crocodiles everywhere. Our roaring engine was an incomprehensible intrusion.

All these creatures scattered and vanished as we flew over them, but it did not seem to be the automatic fear that overtakes herds that are regularly hunted. It was, rather, a bewildered and dumbfounded panic, the sort of reaction human beings have when confronted by some sudden and monstrous reversal in nature, such as an earthquake or a tornado rushing out of a clear sky. At all events these animals soon got over their fright: directly the hellish and inexplicable noise had gone by, they emerged again and began feeding as though nothing had happened.

Presently we reached a place where an electronic device had been set up to gauge the speed and the rise and fall of the current, and here we put down on a pocket handkerchief of level ground beside the river. The helicopter blades ran to a stop as we stepped out, and at once one was absorbed into the silence and the immensity of the gorge. The air was thick and hot, and the surrounding bush growing up the steep sides of the cliff had that curious stillness and completeness that rests on places that have never been disturbed by man. Down in the Sudan and

Egypt one fears the diseases in the broad and placid water of the Nile—bilharzia and the guinea worm, the danger of blindness—but here, in this untouched racing stream, we were able to bathe and drink, and provided one avoided the pools there was no real reason to worry about the crocodiles. And so all day from the point where the Guder River comes into the Nile we buzzed upstream like a gadfly, dropping down on sandbanks where there was something interesting to see, and then on again over hidden bends in the river where the valley widened out and where an occasional village, cut off from all the world, scraped a living from a threadbare crop of maize.

It was not exactly shut in in the gorge—at many places its sides at the top were ten or fifteen miles apart—but it created a certain dullness and uneasiness in the mind, a feeling that it was not natural for one to be there, that one had somehow got oneself involved in one of Conan Doyle's stories of lost worlds, of nameless, unknown swamps and valleys inhabited by the pterodactyl and the dinosaur. A sort of timelessness was in the air, and one looked up occasionally to the clear sky above with a sense of relief.

When eventually the suspension bridge on the Debra Markos road came into view—this one sign of man in so many hundreds of miles of primitive wilderness—it was a slight shock, an anticlimax such as one sometimes experiences on emerging from a dark room into the clear prosaic light of day. We turned up a tributary then until we were confronted by a waterfall that descended in almost vertical cascades from the heights above. Rising up in front of the white rush of spray we regained the plateau and flew back uneventfully to Addis Ababa. It had been a superficial glimpse, of course, but in this one day we had seen things which had taken the early explorers eight years of journeying to reach.

INDEX

INDEX

INDEX

INDEX

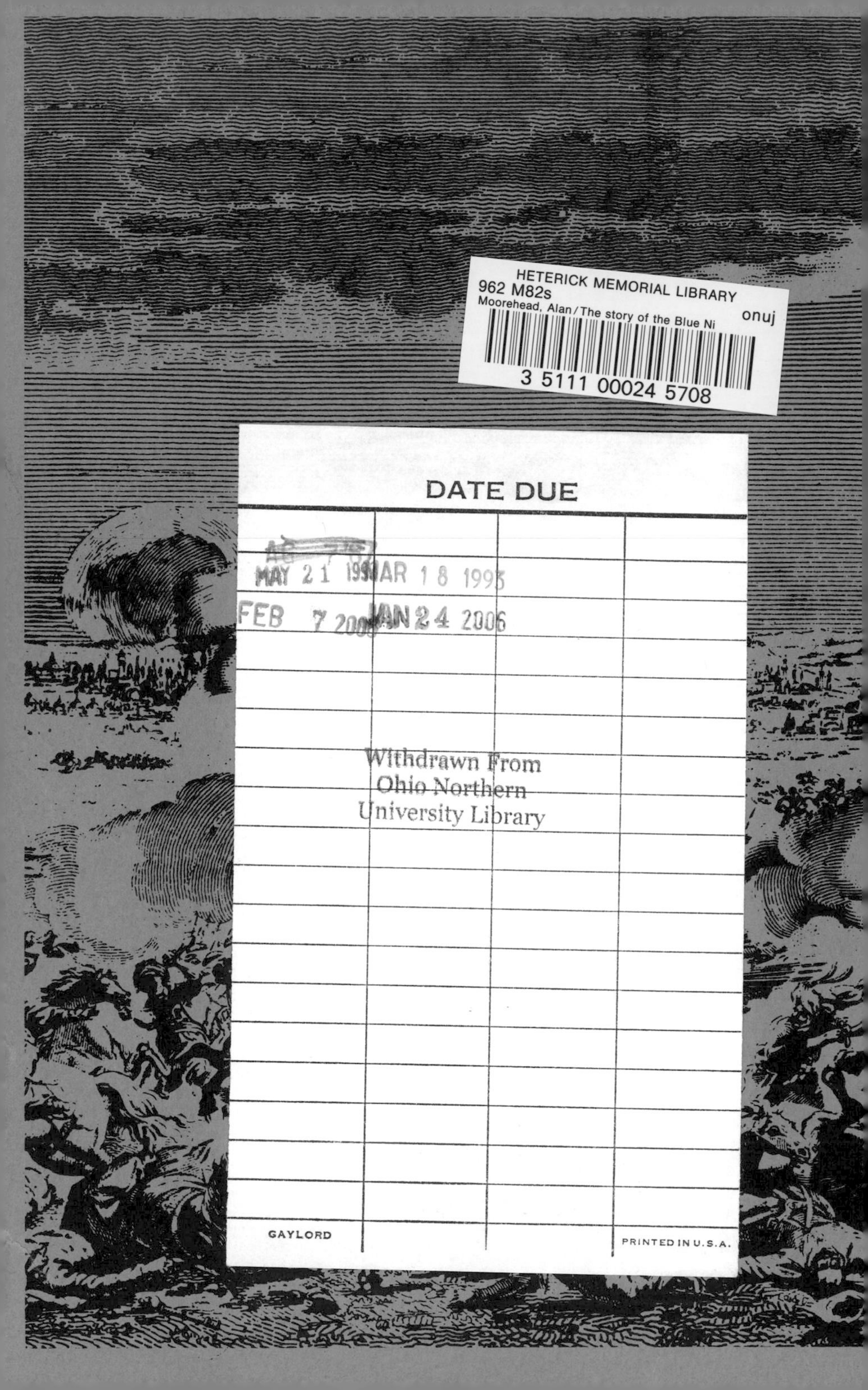